Portland's PAST

Portland's PAST

Stories from the City by the Sea

LUANN YETTER

THE History PRESS

Published by The History Press
Charleston, SC 29403
www.historypress.net

Cover image: Painting by Sara Tarbox, ink and watercolor. *Illustration at top courtesy of the Portland Public Library. Mural courtesy of RiRa Irish Pub.*

First published 2011

Manufactured in the United States

ISBN 978.1.60949.165.9

Yetter, Luann.
Portland's past : stories from the city by the sea / Luann Yetter.
p. cm.
Includes bibliographical references and index.
ISBN 978-1-60949-165-9
1. Portland (Me.)--History--Anecdotes. I. Title.
F29.P9Y48 2011
974.1'91--dc23
2011040351

Contents

CONTENTS

Acknowledgements

Many thanks to Kate Johnson, Amanda Reynolds-Gregg, Sara Tarbox, Abraham Schechter and the staff at the Portland Room of the Public Library and, especially, to Frank Underkuffler.

Author's note: Direct quotes from individuals in the following stories have only been used when there is documentation for them.

Visit the author at luannyetter.com.

George Cleeve Stands His Ground

Cleeve v. Winter

George Cleeve looked John Winter defiantly in the eye and said, "I will be tenant to never a man in New England!"

With that, he and his small party abandoned their log home at Spurwink and sailed north along the coast to a promising-looking inlet. The bay was sheltered, the water calm and the sea breeze bracing. They went ashore at the foot of a hill; to the west was another hill, and a brook ran through the valley in between. It was March 1633 when Cleeve and his companions stood on a piece of land that would one day become a vibrant city. The early spring held promise.

The four refugees—Cleeve; his partner, Richard Tucker; his wife, Joan; and their teenage daughter, Elizabeth—set to work building another log cabin, clearing land and planting corn. Scarcely two years before, they had suffered through the same backbreaking work at the mouth of the River Spurwink. Cleeve had laid legal claim to that land only to have John Winter come along and claim it under a patent from Robert Trelawney. When Winter told him that he had to start paying rent, Cleeve refused. He hadn't uprooted his family and sailed three thousand miles from the comforts of Plymouth, England, to pay rent on wilderness.

Cleeve claimed that Winter had forced him from Spurwink by threat of violence. Winter downplayed the conflict, maintaining that he told Cleeve "in a friendly manner" to leave. Winter didn't want trouble with Cleeve. "Though I have given him warning to depart," he told his boss, Trelawney,

"The Approach of Cleeve and Tucker" (1633). From *Centennial Celebration*, editor John T. Hull (1886).

"I am desirous to live quiet here among the neighbors hereabout, if I may, considering we live here among the heathens." There were enough perils in the new land as it was, and Winter had little reason to needlessly antagonize a fellow Englishman.

It was a land of exotic natives and harsh winters. The new settlers who arrived by ship from across the Atlantic were independent types who had chosen to leave civilization behind for a place to call their own. Once settled here, they found themselves needing to stick to together for the sake of survival. As Cleeve built his new log cabin on a more northern part of Casco Bay, he hoped that his conflicts with Winter were over. Winter had reason to hope the same. They were both wrong.

The feud that began on the River Spurwink in the summer of 1632 would continue for the rest of their lives. It played out on a little neck of land in Casco Bay, but it was as big as all New England and full of Royalist conspiracies and Puritan plots.

Meanwhile, Cleeve planted corn and built a new cabin in a spot at the foot of a hill sheltered from the worst of the northern winds. All in all, it was a better spot than the one from which he had been ousted. This time, he felt confident that he could take legitimate ownership under the royal proclamation that gave every settler 150 acres. Cleeve worked the farm,

"Cleeve and Tucker" (1633). From *Portland and Vicinity*, by Edward Elwell (1876).

while Tucker traded with the Abenaki natives for beaver and otter pelts and shipped them to Massachusetts for cash or provisions, such as worsted stockings or leather shoes, which the settlers couldn't make for themselves. Without a son of his own, Cleeve was grateful for Tucker's partnership.

The winters were severe, but game, fowl and fish were plentiful and the fur trade was profitable. Cleeve knew that he wanted to secure his claim and felt it prudent to make the arduous journey back to England to meet with Ferdinando Gorges, the aristocrat who held the patent on an unfathomably huge section of land between the Piscataqua and Kennebec Rivers. In England, Cleeve was the diplomat, ingratiating himself to Royalist Gorges while at the same time speaking well of John Winthrop, the Puritan governor of Massachusetts. His efforts were successful, and he returned to Casco Bay with more than he could have hoped for. He had increased the size of his claim more than tenfold, leasing 1,500 acres from Gorges for one hundred pounds. The lease, for an unusually long one thousand years, proclaimed that the land was "now and forever from henceforth to be called or known by the name Stogummor." When Cleeve returned to the Neck, far away from the whims and influence of Gorges, he forgot all about the new name. The valuable piece of real estate he now held was never called "Stogummor."

Cleeve also had Gorges's commission to act as his land agent, "letting and settling all or any part of his lands or islands lying between the Cape Elizabeth and the entrance of Sagadahock [Kennebec] River, and so up into the main land sixty miles."

Meanwhile, on Richmond Island, Cleeve's coup did not sit well with John Winter. "Sir Ferdinand Gorges hath made Cleeve governor of his province, as he reports," he complained to Trelawney. "Now he thinks to wind all men to his will."

Cleeve wasn't Winter's only problem; he had some explaining to do to his proprietor. Trelawney had heard "ill reports" about Winter's wife beating her maid. Treating the maid fairly had gotten no results, Winter explained in his wife's defense. "If a fair way will not work," he wrote, "beating must, sometimes, upon such idle girls as she is." The maid, who had been around for more than two years, was no doubt an indentured servant. Treated much like a slave, she had tried to escape. "She has twice gone marching in the woods," he said. "We can hardly keep her indoors after we've gone to bed, except we carry the key of the door to bed with us." Winter had any number of complaints about the maid: she couldn't learn how to milk a cow or goat, she wouldn't slop the pigs, she slept with her clothes on and "she is so fat and soggy she can hardly do any work…she is so slutty that our men do not desire to have her boil the kettle for them." Winter was quick to come to his wife's defense: "If this maid at her lazy times, when she's been found wrong

"Cleeve and Tucker Building the First Log House" (1633). From *Centennial Celebration*.

in her actions, does not deserve two or three blows, I pray judge you who has more right to complain, my wife or the maid."

Winter's wife was not popular with Cleeve, either. When she still lived in Plymouth, Cleeve had called her "the veriest drunkenest whore in all that town." This piece of information was revisited in 1640 when the first court was held in the province. The settlers flocked to the official proceedings, ready to vent years of pent-up frustrations. When the court opened for business, Winter sued Cleeve for slander, claiming that he and his wife had been "greatly prejudiced in their reputation" due to the terrible things that Cleeve had said about her.

Meanwhile, in another suit heard during the flurry of lawsuits, Cleeve had plenty to say about Winter, who, according to Cleeve, was determined to uproot him again. "Moved with envy and for some other sinister cause," Cleeve claimed, "he hath now for these three years past, and still doth unjustly pretend an interest and thereupon hath and doth still interrupt me to my great hindrance, thereby seeking my ruin and utter overthrow."

Winter countered that Cleeve "cunningly and fraudulently by false information obtained the…lease" to his property. The court decided in Cleeve's favor on this one, confirming his leasehold. As for the slander against his wife, Winter enjoyed a symbolic victory. Cleeve was ordered to "Christianly acknowledge his failing therein against Mr. Winter his and afterwards to Mrs. Winter."

As one of the more prominent men in northern New England, Winter was a popular defendant. He also came under fire from some of the trappers in the area for bringing down the price of beaver. South of Winter's Richmond Island, traders had been paying eight shillings for beaver pelt, but Winter insisted on paying only six shillings, and now the other traders were following his lead. Winter was driving the price down, and the trappers were hurting. Not only was Winter trying to deflate the price of beaver, but they claimed that he was also overcharging for liquor. He paid seven pounds for a hogshead of brandy and then turned around and sold it for thirty-three pounds. Without a lot of trading posts along the wild northern New England shore, the trappers didn't think it was fair to force such high prices and low compensation. The court, however, must have felt that free trade should be upheld, because it sided with Winter in the case of the liquor and beavers.

In 1642, civil war broke out in England, and Royalists were shocked to find their monarchy challenged. Trelawney, the powerful patent holder of Maine's land and member of the English Parliament, was thrown in prison for his loyalty to the Crown. Gorges, the holder of an even bigger patent in New England, was in exile with the king. Almost overnight, the rules changed. Puritans in England were gaining power, and Cleeve knew that it was time to return to the fatherland to align himself with the new order. He sailed to England out of Boston on a ship laden with Virginian tobacco and arranged a meeting with Parliamentarian Alexander Rigby. Exercising his diplomatic skills once again, Cleeve convinced Rigby to buy the patent that included his land and the land occupied by Winter and others. Cleeve also convinced Rigby to make him deputy governor. With the upheaval in England, Cleeve's new authority was more theoretical than actual. The possibility of Trelawney returning to power died with him in prison in 1644, and Cleeve's position against Winter was strengthened. The next year, his longtime foe, John Winter, died on Richmond Island.

Cleeve and Winter had both lived hard lives, battling the elements in a raw and uncivilized outpost far from the comforts of urban Plymouth, England. Both men had managed to forge lives for themselves in a world largely beyond the reach of the law. In the end, the contest between Cleeve and Winter ended in a draw. Winter died with his property and reputation intact. Cleeve soon discovered a new foe and fought on.

CLEEVE V. JORDAN

To George Cleeve, Reverend Robert Jordan was "a minister of the Anti-Christ." An ordained Episcopal minister, Jordan was educated at Oxford and closely aligned with the Church of England. Anti-Christ or man of God, his interests were definitely temporal as well as spiritual. Despite his calling, Jordan seemed eager to get his hands on all the Casco Bay property he could. He began by marrying John Winter's daughter, Sarah. With John Winter's death, Jordan took his place on Richmond Island. He then started harassing George Cleeve.

As patent holder Alexander Rigby's land agent, Cleeve appealed to Governor John Winthrop in 1645 on behalf of several landowners who had recently received their land under Rigby's patent. He complained dramatically that "we are in great distress by a company of factious men who have leagued themselves together to murder us." Their problem lay with a man named Vines, another land manager in the area, and Jordan. "From these two men," Cleeve wrote, "all this evil doth principally flow." Cleeve said that Jordan and Vines were turning citizens against him and his followers. Jordan and Vines used depositions from people who "accuse some of us falsely and slanderously with treason and other crimes…Thus we are all destined to them unto destruction, if the Lord prevent not their wicked plots against us."

On the other side of the Atlantic, Englishmen were rebelling against King Charles I and were in the throes of their first civil war. The temper of the times there had clearly influenced the inhabitants of Casco Bay. Given its close ties to the fatherland, their small New World could be next. Jordan and Vines had rebellious intent. Cleeve warned Winthrop that their next court proceedings would be dangerous. His opponents "intend to make this the beginning of Civil War, which they intend to blow abroad into all parts of this land."

Governor Winthrop calmly responded to Cleeve with an understatement: "We perceive that the differences between you are grown to a great height of contention." Winthrop reminded him that the differences needed to be decided by Rigby and others in England. Both the Cleeve and Jordan factions had already written to the patent holders; they simply needed to be patient. "Answer is expected by the first return," he assured them. "Forbear any further contention in the meantime."

In 1648, Cleeve was on a committee that actually issued a decree in Jordan's favor. Representing the estate of his father-in-law, Jordan had sued the estate of Robert Trelawney. Jailed for being a Royalist during the civil war, Trelawney's financial affairs were a mess. When he died in an English prison, his estate was meager. Cleeve's General Assembly was convened to decide Jordan's claim. After much detailed accounting, the assembly determined that Trelawney's estate owed the Winter estate 605 pounds. Jordan was awarded temporary possession of the Richmond Island and Spurwink properties, at least until the Trelawney estate paid up. As the assembly's deputy president, Cleeve signed on to the judgment in Jordan's favor but still managed one parting shot. No doubt on Cleeve's initiative, the panel left the actual ownership of the land Trelawney had claimed undecided. Jordan could occupy it for the time being but was still "left in suspense for want of appearance of any right Mr. Trelawny hath in it." How long "the petitioner shall retain the possession" was left for the courts to decide.

As it turned out, Jordan and his heirs retained "temporary" possession as long as no one challenged their title by the time they finally sold the land themselves. Trelawney's affairs were in such disarray that the 605 pounds were never paid.

Taking possession of Winter's land wasn't enough for Jordan. In an effort to increase his holdings even more, he challenged the Rigby patent on purely

"The Block House" (1689). From *Centennial Celebration*.

technical grounds. This challenge unsettled everyone claiming under Rigby, including everyone in the area now known as Casco Neck. Their titles in jeopardy, these residents collaborated on a letter to the General Court in 1660, asking it to take the settlers' plight "into serious consideration." They beseeched the General Court to side with Cleeve because if it backed Jordan, "no man shall enjoy what he hath labored upon and possessed."

The following year, Cleeve petitioned the court to form a committee to settle the dispute. Not merely content to lay claim to Cleeve's land, Reverend Jordan was also agitating Cleeve's tenants "by means whereof the populating of the town of Falmouth is much hindered to the great loss and detriment of your petitioner and considerable hindrance to the country." Jordan had been plaguing him for years with frivolous lawsuits, he said, and "if help and redress fail, he is in a fair way able to ruin your humble petitioner."

Jordan was a generation younger than Cleeve, but he showed no respect to his elder. By 1663, Cleeve was at least in his late sixties or early seventies, and Jordan was still "vexing" him as much as he could. When his effort to seize all of Cleeve's land stalled, Jordan concentrated his energies on lesser issues. Claiming that Cleeve owed him money, Jordan sent a constable to collect it. According to Cleeve, Jordan's constable invaded his home and made off with nearly everything he owned, "house, cow, bed and bolster and bed clothes, my brewing kettle, pot and other goods." Anything he did not take, the constable simply threw out of the house—"all my other goods, as apparel, chests, trunks and provisions…who so acted to the spoiling and breaking of many of my things to my damage more than a hundred pounds sterling." Cleeve claimed that the deputy constable's accomplice, who was very drunk, took an open kettle of beer and dumped it all over the house. Worst of all, the two thugs entered his wife's bedroom, where she lay sick, pulled the bed out from under her and carried it away. Cleeve claimed that Jordan intended no less than to "starve and ruin" him.

Meanwhile, Jordan was having his own problems. With Puritan Oliver Cromwell ruling England, Massachusetts was flexing its own Puritan muscles in New England and had a tight hold on the province of Maine. Robert Jordan, as a fervent Episcopal minister, was not a favorite of the Puritans. In 1654, he was indicted for renouncing the authority of the Puritan Commonwealth and jailed in Boston.

In 1660, the political tide shifted once again with the restoration of the monarchy in England, and Puritan rule there ended with finality. As usual, the events in England rippled across the Atlantic. The Restoration was good for Jordan, who would no longer need to worry about getting thrown in jail for his Episcopal sentiments or sympathy toward the Church of England. In 1664, Charles II abrogated the authority of Massachusetts in the provinces and sent a group of commissioners to oversee Maine directly. While in theory this looked good for Jordan and his interests, the commissioners were so ineffective that they made little real difference. Once established in New England, they seem to have been forgotten by the Crown. With no support from the fatherland, the commissioners of the king and their authority were gone within three years, and the Commonwealth of Massachusetts was more firmly in power than ever in the provinces.

Having devoted his entire adult life to defending his real estate against one claimant after another, George Cleeve passed away in 1666. Perhaps he would not be surprised to learn that the land he fought so desperately to keep eventually became the thriving city of Portland. He never faltered in his defense of it, and we can assume that he never faltered in his love for that valley, brook and two rounded hills sloping into the protected harbor in Casco Bay.

Robert Jordan was eventually defeated by a foe deadlier than George Cleeve, Oliver Cromwell or any of the Puritans of New England. In the wake of the first devastating Indian war, he fled from Casco Bay in terror just before the natives set fire to his home. He never returned.

Thou Has Slain Thy Child

The corpse was brought into the courtroom and shown to Mary Martin. The infant had been dead for a few days, and the crowd watched anxiously. Mary was forced to reach her hand out to her dead daughter. "When she touched the face of it before the jury, the blood came fresh into it," reported Reverend Cotton Mather.

Mary Martin was found guilty.

Mary had been raised in the genteel society of Plymouth, England, where the Martin family was well respected and well established. Yet Mary's father, Francis, was never the most successful of the clan, and as he grew older his merchant fortunes declined. His wife died and his health suffered. Francis hoped that his future, and the future of his two daughters, might be brighter in New England. They sailed across the Atlantic and arrived in Casco Bay in 1640. The trading outpost they found on Richmond Island was more rustic than anything they had ever seen. Mary and her sister had been raised in a world of needlework and parlor rooms, Francis in a world of gentleman merchants. None of them was prepared for the harsh realities of a subsistence lifestyle.

"I know not how he will live here well," mused John Winter to his proprietor, Robert Trelawney, as he helped Francis settle. "He hath never a servant, and he cannot work himself, and here is nothing to be gotten without hard labor."

Winter's fears were well founded. The family had to depend on Winter for their provisions, and he sent the bill to Francis's nephew in Plymouth. Francis eventually managed to cultivate a little corn, but that's almost all the family had to eat. "He is in a bad way of living here with his two children,"

Winter remarked of Martin few years later. "His children are not brought up to work, so I know not what shift he will make to live."

In 1646, Francis sailed back to England, probably with financial help from his nephew, where he hoped to put his financial affairs in better order. He left his single daughters in the care of Michael and Elizabeth Mitton.

Elizabeth had lived on Casco Neck since her childhood, when she arrived with her father, George Cleeve, who laid claim to the land and built the first shelter. After a business trip back to England, her father brought Michael Mitton back with him. Like Cleeve, Winter and others, Mitton was from Plymouth, England. He had been raised a gentleman but was young and active and seemed suited for an outdoor lifestyle. Elizabeth's marriage to him, part domestic arrangement and part business deal, had surprised no one. Her father had been generous and gave them land to make their own home. They lived on Back Cove, where a few other families had also settled. By the time Mary joined them, they had two young daughters and a third on the way. Mary made herself useful in helping Elizabeth care for the young children. Later that year, when the baby was born, Michael and Elizabeth named their third daughter Mary.

Yet all was not well. Much that happened during those months that Mary was with the Martins was shrouded in secrecy. Behind closed doors and away from the eyes of the other settlers, the conventions of their genteel, faraway Plymouth society broke down completely—and for Mary, irrevocably.

Mary had left Casco and become a servant in Boston before she discovered that she was pregnant with Michael Mitton's child. With no other option, she concealed the pregnancy.

"Did I not think thou wert an honest and sincere creature," her new mistress remarked one day, "I shall verily think thou wert with child?" But Mary continued to deny her condition and managed to deceive her mistress, although others around her had their suspicions. She gave birth alone in a back room at night. Overcome with the mounting hopelessness of her circumstances, she lost her mind. After the labor and delivery, she tried to smother her baby girl.

Yet when she laid her daughter aside for dead, the baby cried. She had to try again to kill the child, and this time she succeeded. Insane with grief and guilt, she hid the corpse in a chest. She cleaned the room, went to bed, got up the next day and resumed her household duties. For six days, no one knew what Mary had done. When her mistress left for England, Mary was forced to find somewhere else to live. Away from the protection of her mistress, she was confronted by a midwife who had been suspicious of her behavior. Mary denied giving birth. She denied ever being pregnant, but the midwife pressed her for an admission.

"The Skiff." From *With Pen and Ink: In and About Portland* (compiled 1897).

The child had been stillborn, Mary said, and she had burned the body. It was the inconsistencies in Mary's stories that kept the midwife suspicious, and Mary's room was searched. Her accusers found the corpse, and Mary's worst secrets were revealed.

There is an old wives' tale that a murderer's touch will revive the one he or she murdered. Witnesses said that the blood returned to the baby's face when Mary was forced to touch her in court that day. A surgeon was brought in to examine the corpse and testified that the skull had been fractured. Mary was found guilty and sentenced to death.

The trial attracted much attention in seventeenth-century Boston, and many Puritans endeavored to save Mary's soul before her life was taken. They prayed that she might be renewed by repentance. Inspired by the event, Cotton Mather of Boston's North Church preached a sermon from Ezekiel: "Is this of thy whoredoms a small matter that thou has slain my children?"

"It was hoped that these endeavors were not lost," Mather reported later. "Her carriage in her imprisonment and at her execution was very penitent," he said hopefully. Just before they hanged her, Mary admitted that she thought she had succeeded in killing her child only to find it still alive, so she had to try a second time before the baby was really dead. When they hanged Mary Martin, they failed to kill her the first time. They had to hang her again before she died.

Back on Casco Bay, Michael Mitton and his wife had three more children. People said that he liked to hunt birds and was quite a "fowler." In social gatherings, he took pleasure in telling tall tales. He lived peacefully on Casco Neck until his death in 1660. He never had to answer for the sad fate of the young girl who had once been in his care.

A More Dangerous Enemy

A Bold Move

Simon was tall, his smock decorated with beads and porcupine quills and his dark eyes flashing. "It must be," he said. "Would you rather serve us or be slain by us?" Ann Mitton knew that she was about to lose the place she called home.

Ann had spent her whole life in the small settlement on Casco Bay called the Neck. As she was growing up, the land was alternately under the jurisdiction of the king of England and the Massachusetts Commonwealth. That meant that either the Episcopalians or the Puritans were holding sway in her little village, but who wielded political power at any given time didn't matter much to Ann. When she was growing up, she never felt very threatened by the Indians. They lived on the perimeter of her world, with a language and customs too different for her to understand.

As a girl, helping her mother with the housework and caring for the younger children had occupied her time. Mills in the area ground corn for bread, and visitors said that they were lucky to have such plentiful provisions; a rotation of beef, pork, mutton, fowl and fish graced the dinner table night after night. Meeting new people had always been a fun pastime. Ann had watched families come into the area every year since she was a little girl. Ann's parents had come from Plymouth, England, but most of the new settlers had come to the Neck from Massachusetts or the province of New Hampshire. They wore the dark colors of the Puritans, and the young ones, like Ann, did not remember the fatherland. Their world was the New World, and while their parents might have reminisced about the lovely towns and bustling cities of England, for Ann a land so crowded with people was hard to even imagine.

Coming from one of the early English families, Ann was a good catch. Thanks to her grandfather, George Cleeve, marriage to Ann or one of her sisters would come with a dowry of desirable land. When Anthony Brackett and his brother arrived from New Hampshire to settle on the Neck, the attractiveness of the Mitton sisters was not lost on them. Anthony married Ann, and Thomas married her sister, Mary.

Anthony was a hard worker, and he eventually added to his property until he had four hundred acres along Back Cove. Ann and Anthony were prosperous enough to have servants, including a black farmhand. Anthony was well respected in the community and in 1665 was chosen as constable of Falmouth. This was a duty that included not just the Neck but many of the surrounding settlements as well. A few years later, he became a commissioner for the town. As the years went by, Ann gave birth to five children. Life was good, both active and fruitful.

The white population grew, but Ann and her neighbors never considered what their numbers meant to the natives. More and more settlers populated their lands and threatened the life that they had always known. The newcomers maintained their complacency in the land they called New England until an Indian leader called King Phillip organized Indians in Massachusetts and tensions erupted in war.

In 1675, word reached the Neck of Indian uprisings to the south, and settlers began to feel afraid. In September, Indians broke into the house of Thomas Purchase not far north of Falmouth and stole his liquor and ammunition. A few days later, some white hunters killed an Indian in the cornfields on the north end of Casco Bay with little provocation. In retaliation, the Indians wounded several of the settlers and stole two boats full of their corn.

These encounters made Ann feel increasingly insecure, but the real terror began when she heard the fate of her neighbors, the Wakelys. No one knew why the massacre was focused on this family. The gruesome sight that awaited the first visitor when he came upon the bodies of the four adults and four children was one that he didn't care to describe in the company of women. Ann's life, never an easy one but always a relatively secure one, was now turned upside down.

She watched as many of her friends and neighbors left Falmouth for the safety of more populous places like Salem and Boston. Yet Ann couldn't imagine leaving the place that had always been her home. Anthony and

"By the Seaside." From *The Complete Poetical Works of Henry Wadsworth Longfellow* (1884).

Ann determined to stay. Anthony was on good terms with some of the neighboring Indians, including Simon, a newcomer to the area who seemed like the God-fearing sort. The Brackett family thought of him as one of the "praying Indians," little suspecting that he was a recent escapee from Dover prison or that his nickname was "Simon the Yankee Killer."

The year after the terrible Wakely massacre, with the Indian war still raging in some areas around New England, Simon arrived at the Brackett house with a group of Abenakis. Blind to their motives, Anthony let them into his house. Once inside, he realized his terrible mistake when the Indians quickly started rounding up all the guns they could find.

"What is the meaning of this?" Anthony asked Simon frantically.

"It must be," said Simon. "Would you rather serve us or be slain by us?"

With his family surrounding him, Anthony had only one answer. "I would rather serve you than be killed by you," he said with resignation.

The Indians proceeded to bind the wrists of all their white captives, including Anthony, Ann, four of their five children, their black servant and Ann's brother, Nathaniel. Nathaniel resisted, and the Indians' reaction was swift and brutal. Ann watched helplessly as he died. With baby Kezia in her arms, she could do nothing as the Indians burned her house and all of her material possessions. The wooden furniture, the woolen clothing, the earthenware pottery and more went up in flames.

The Brackett house was only the first one attacked that day. The family was forced to go along with the Indians as they went on a rampage, from one dwelling to another, killing about a dozen settlers and setting fire to their homes. Ann watched as her brother-in-law, Thomas, was also killed. Her sister, Mary, and Mary's children were taken captive, along with a dozen other friends and neighbors.

Anthony and Ann's children, all but the baby still in her arms, were mercifully left behind when the Indians decided to leave the Neck and head toward the Kennebec River. Anthony, Ann and their servant were taken by force as far as Arrowsic Island. There they heard from other Indians of the capture of a house along the Kennebec that would yield great stores of guns, furs and liquor. The Indians were eager to get there and share in the spoils. In an effort to motivate the Bracketts to keep up, they promised their captives a share in the goods and then hurried ahead of them.

Ann was desperate to return to her children, who had been abandoned on the Neck, and she was ready to do anything to get back home. As the Indians got farther ahead, Ann managed to find two answers to her prayers: an old, ripped birch-bark canoe and a needle. Desperately, she went to work mending the canoe with her needle and whatever she could find for thread. With the baby and the servant, the group launched the canoe and took to the water. The August winds were light and in their favor. Miraculously, they managed to cross Casco Bay without sinking and arrived safely at Black Point unharmed. There they were rescued by a boat bound for the relative safety of the Piscataqua River. Ann's prayers were answered and her efforts rewarded. She was reunited with her children.

Ann's sister, Mary, died in her first year of captivity with the Indians. Her three children survived and somehow found refuge far away in Greenland. Other families who were taken captive that day spent two long years as prisoners of war but were eventually released as part of the terms of a peace treaty. Many of them returned to Falmouth.

Ann's bravery had allowed her to escape captivity, but her home and possessions had been burned to ash, her land parched by flame, stained with blood and occupied by the enemy. She, Anthony and the children were forced to relocate farther south to wait out the Indian war. Her ordeal had taken much out of Ann and living conditions in war-ravaged New England were wretched. She died before the resettlement and never saw Casco Neck again.

A Dream in Ashes

Seth Brackett died at Fort Loyal in 1690, but no one was there to dig a grave or say a prayer for him.

Fourteen years before, Seth had been just a child when his home on Casco Neck had been invaded by the enemy. He had witnessed the Abenakis kill two of his uncles, burn his house down and take his parents prisoner. If it hadn't been for their cunning escape in an old birch-bark canoe, they would have been lost to him in Canada.

Reuniting with his parents provided some comfort after the terror of the Indian attack, but life was hard when they were forced to leave the farm for a safer settlement farther south. The family missed their home, as well as the independence and bounty that went with it.

The Indian leader, King Phillip, was dead. Seth heard stories of the Puritans proudly displaying his head on a stake in Plymouth. In the province of Maine, Simon the Yankee Killer and his comrades were still waging war. During the bitterly cold of the winter of 1677, there was a skirmish at Brunswick. In the spring, three English were killed at Black Point, and soon after that the Brackett family heard that Simon had attacked Wells and York, killing seven and taking two captive. There was no point in thinking about a return to their beloved farm. Seth, his four siblings and his parents lived as refugees, a life that took its toll on Seth's mother, Ann, who died within a year of her great escape. Seth's father, Anthony, struggled to care for his five children, and it wasn't long before he enlisted help by way of a new wife.

Finally, in April 1678, better news reached the Brackett family. In their own town of Falmouth, a treaty had been signed. Squanto, Madockawando and other Abenaki leaders had met with three Massachusetts-appointed commissioners. An agreement had been reached. Captives would be returned, and settlers would begin to pay the Indian confederation a quit-rent—a peck of corn from every family, every year.

With the immediate threat of attack gone, the refugees were eager to cease living on the charity of others and return home. Seth, his brother and their three sisters returned to their farmland with their father and new stepmother. For the second time, Anthony built a house west of Back Cove and settled in. Reuniting with old friends and neighbors was bittersweet, but soon the town was buzzing with activity as exiles and captives returned to again build, clear, plant and fish. The government built Fort Loyal near the bay, and the added protection allowed the settlers to feel secure. Anthony's status in the community remained, and he was appointed lieutenant of Falmouth, which put him in charge of the fort. Within the next ten years, Seth grew to manhood, and he acquired five new half-brothers and sisters. Seth's grandmother, Elizabeth, died in 1682. Her stories of the earliest days on the Neck, when she lived there alone with just her mother and father and Richard Tucker, began to feel like myths as the community grew to about twenty-five families.

The quit-rent due to their Indian neighbors was easy to forget. No one wanted to do without a peck of corn, and the requirement faded in the settlers' minds. The white people of Maine were not holding up their part of the treaty, a breach of promise that was not lost on the Abenakis. Meanwhile, French missionaries to the north and east had become more influential with the natives. In North America, the French were bitterly hostile to the English. Each side jealously guarded the land they had claimed in the New World, as well as the profitable fur trade derived from it. In 1688, the Nine Year's War began in Europe with France's Louis XIV waging conflict against the Grand Alliance, which included England.

On the other side of the Atlantic, war was also brewing. The Bracketts began to hear stories of Indians killing settlers' cattle nearby. In Saco, the authorities arrested several Indians for being "cruel and murderous rogues," and they were imprisoned right on the Neck in Fort Loyal. In September, there was a battle in North Yarmouth, and in the summer of 1689, the French and Penobscot took Pemaquid. All of the inhabitants fled to Fort Loyal with stories of the attack.

With danger mounting, the settlers knew that their fort was undermanned and underarmed. They were relieved when Massachusetts sent Major Benjamin Church with a troop of volunteer soldiers. The settlers had heard of Church; his expedition against King Phillip had resulted in the Indian leader's death.

By the time Church and his troop arrived, the Indians were closing in and had landed on Peak's Island. The Indians paddled from the island to the Neck in the dark and invaded at dawn. Seth Brackett awoke to the awful memory of the terror he had felt as a child. The Indians were back on the Brackett farm, and the bloody battle ensued in their orchard. When the Indians retreated, eleven of the English, both soldiers and settlers, were dead. Among the dead was Seth's father, Anthony, whose long battle with the native enemy came to an end on the farm he had fought so desperately to defend.

The enemy was gone, but residents on the Neck did not breathe a sigh of relief. They felt sure that the Indians would return in the spring, and many considered retreating again to safer places in the south. Major Church persuaded them to stay and said that he would return with troops for their defense in the spring. Church wanted to be good on his word and spent the winter trying to convince the government of Massachusetts that his return was necessary, but his opinion fell on deaf ears. The settlers were given no soldiers to help in their defense.

No regular troops were at the fort or the four garrison houses in the area when spring came. Silvanus Davis had taken Seth's father's place as the local commander of the fort. Word came to the Brackett farm that Indians had been spotted and that they had French reinforcements with them. The Brackett family, along with many of their neighbors, fled to the garrison houses. About thirty of the men left the safety of the garrisons to scout the area. The enemy found them on Munjoy Hill, and the ensuing Indian attack left fourteen settlers killed. The Indians targeted the garrison houses next. The settlers tried to fight them off in a conflict that continued throughout the day. When the battle ended with the coming of the night, settlers fled in secrecy to Fort Loyal, where they had more ammunition and provisions to hold off the enemy.

Seth could smell smoke when he woke in the morning. He tried to fight off the childhood memories of his farm in flames. As the settlers looked out of the seaside fort windows, they could see flames rising in every direction and smoke billowing from every homestead.

They were outnumbered five to one, but they had nowhere to go, no way to escape and only the hope that reinforcements would come. The French and Indians dug a trench to avoid the cannon fire and were determined to wait out their captives.

For five days, the settlers held off the enemy, but supplies were getting low and waiting any longer would mean starvation. Davis and the others in the fort suspected that French soldiers were among the four or five hundred enemy combatants. "We demanded if there were any French among them," said Davis. Thinking that the French would be easier to negotiate with, the settlers were relieved to hear they were there. "We sent out to them…to know if they would give us good quarter," said Davis, "both for our men, women and children, both wounded and sound, and that we should have liberty to march to the next English town." Davis asked that the French commander "hold up his hand and swear by the great and ever living God, that the several articles should be performed. All which he did solemnly swear to perform."

Physically exhausted and emotionally defeated, Davis, Seth, his brother and their neighbors began to trudge out of the fort, into the bracing spring winds and toward the enemy. Safe passage was nowhere in sight. In an act of betrayal and treachery, the French seized the settlers—men, women and children.

"As soon as they had us in their custody," Davis reported, "they broke their articles, suffered our women and children and our men to be made captives in the hands of the heathen, to be cruelly murdered and destroyed many of them, and especially our wounded men."

Five they took captive, including Davis and Seth's older brother. Seth and the rest were slaughtered, leaving safe passage for no one.

The cries, prayers and screams that day were loud and terrible, but eventually the French and Indians paddled away, leaving the fort empty and the town in ruins. The human voices could no longer be heard. On the ground near the shore, the brutalized bodies of the settlers lay still. And so they remained through that summer as no one, soldier or civilian, English, French or Indian, returned to the Neck. The hot sun beat down on the bodies; the animals found them. In the fall, the dead leaves blew around them, and in the winter, they froze and were covered with snow. When spring came, the cycle started again.

And so the scene remained for two years, until Major Church and his troops came upon them, dug graves for the bones and said prayers. The soldiers soon left, and all was silent again. No human voice could be heard at the grave site or among the charred remains of the dwellings. The years went by. The wild animals prowled and foraged, and the brush and trees reclaimed the fields. The fishing boats rotted on the shore. For twenty-six years, the Neck flourished in its natural state, completely abandoned of human habitation.

The Rebels and the Parent State

Nor Any Other Power on Earth

Jedediah Preble, Esquire, and his wife, Martha, made a fine couple when they appeared on the streets of Casco Neck. Jedediah's scarlet coat and lace hat were striking with his height and military bearing; Martha's lace fichu marked them as members of the privileged class.

They were Falmouth's newest addition, young and ambitious, and in 1748, the town welcomed them as one more sign that Falmouth was secure and prosperous once again. The town's revival had begun gradually. An entire generation passed before anyone returned to the area that had been so thoroughly devastated during the Indian wars. In 1716, a few of the old families began to reclaim their property, and a few new people began to buy up leases. They cleared land again and built with the hope that they would be free from attack this time. Within a few years, twenty families lived on the Neck, and even more people dwelled in the outlying areas. Together they incorporated and called their town Falmouth.

By the time Preble invested in Falmouth, it was a thriving seaport of about five hundred families. He bought property on the Neck, where access to the harbor was easiest and property values highest. He and Martha settled in with their five young children. Within a few years, he was representing Falmouth in the General Court, but Martha did not live to see her children become adults. In 1753, she passed away at the age of thirty-nine. Left with the responsibility for his sons and daughters, forty-seven-year-old Jedediah quickly married Mehetable Bangs Roberts, a young and childless widow of twenty-six. Their first baby was a girl, and they named her Martha.

Preble was a military man, and he was often gone on expeditions for long periods of time. Whenever war erupted across the Atlantic between England and France, tensions built between the English and French provinces in North America. In 1755, he was part of the force that expelled the Acadians from their home in Canada, some of them coming to Falmouth for refuge. Preble was on the Plains of Abraham for the English victory in 1759. When word reached the Neck a month later, townspeople celebrated by firing cannons, illuminating ships in the harbor and observing a day of thanksgiving. Falmouth felt secure from its enemies.

The Neck was fast becoming an important port. British ships laden with timber sailed out of the harbor, bound for the Royal Navy. Schooners full of lumber and fish sailed to the West Indies and came back with sugar cane and its byproducts, molasses and rum. Trade from Falmouth was profitable until 1764, when England began enforcing the Sugar Act. Francis Waldo,

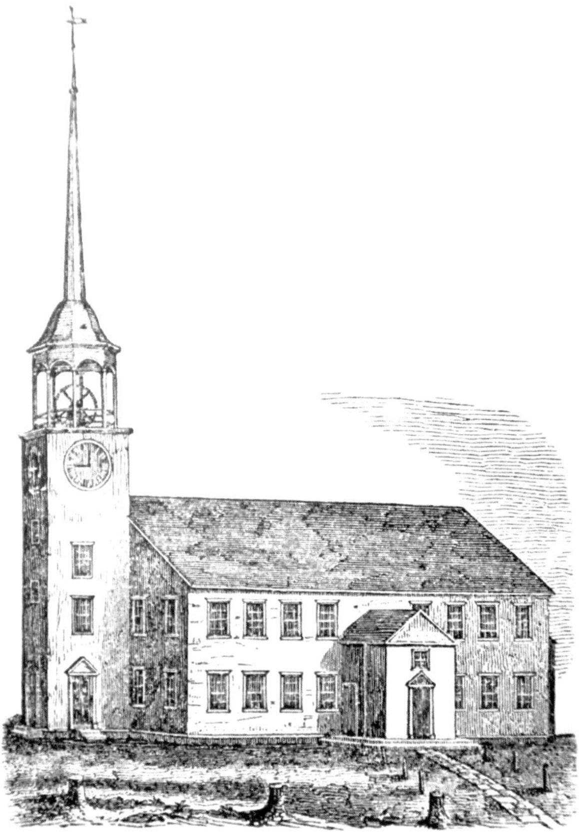

"Meeting House" (1740–1826). From *Portland, ME. First Parish Church: 75th Anniversary* (1901).

appointed by the Crown as the customs officer at the port, became the most unpopular man on the Neck. When he seized Enoch Ilsley's rum and sugar for nonpayment of revenue, residents were outraged. They managed to break into Waldo's residence, took back the goods and hid them from him.

The Stamp Act put more burdens on the colonists. The lower courts ignored the tax, but the customs officers tried to use the stamped paper, which again resulted in a mob scene. The protestors seized the papers with the hated stamp on them, stuck them to the end of a pole, paraded them through town and then burned them amid a cheering crowd. When England repealed the Stamp Act the next year, the people on the Neck celebrated. "Our people are mad with drink and joy," Reverend Samuel Smith noted, "bells ringing, drums beating, colors flying, guns firing, the court house illuminated and some others, a bon fire, and a deluge of drunkenness."

Preble was not part of the mob. As a brigadier general and community leader, he tried to follow the law and felt sure that the province's complaints could be addressed through negotiation. In 1768, he was a representative to the provincial convention that met in opposition to English troops in Boston. Preble was one of the delegates who confirmed his loyalty to the Crown, advised his fellow colonists to act moderately and calmly stated his grievances. In 1770, England repealed all of the acts except the tax on tea. Preble probably counted this as a victory; the people of Falmouth immediately voted a boycott on tea.

As time went on, even some of the more conservative residents of Falmouth grew disillusioned with the English government and their cold response to the provinces. When Bostonians boldly threw English tea into the Massachusetts Bay in 1774, most of the leaders in Falmouth supported them. Preble's resentment toward the Crown was increasing, too. He became one of the founding members of Falmouth's committee of correspondence, whose members declared their conviction that "neither the Parliament of Great Britain nor any other power on earth has a right to lay a tax on us but by our own consent or the consent of those whom we may choose to represent us."

Preble's alliances were shifting in other ways as well. He was from one of the leading families of York in the province of Maine, and his family was, of course, Episcopalian; they had strong ties to the Church of England, to the king and to the old religious traditions that predated Protestantism. As Preble felt the king's disregard for his provincial subjects increasing, he felt those ties to the church loosening. When Falmouth's Episcopalian minister, John Wiswall, persisted in saying prayers for the king and royal family, Preble switched his allegiance to Parson Smith and the First Parish Church. The congregation's roots were with the strict puritanical teachings of the early Plymouth Plantation, but each church held an autonomy that allowed it to respond to the times. Preble found his identity with the First Parish and began taking his family to services in the crude wooden building on King Street.

England was tightening its grip on Massachusetts, and when Parliament took away the province's right to elect its own civil officers, the Massachusetts response was swift and decisive. The citizens formed their own provincial government, and Preble was appointed one of three general officers of the provincial forces.

In December, the Falmouth selectmen removed the cannons, powder, balls and gun carriages from their fort. For more than one hundred years, residents had been England's loyal subjects; they had looked to England for defense, and England's enemies had been their enemies. Now, the people of Falmouth removed the weapons because they wanted to remain in control; they feared that England might use the guns against them.

OUR TOWN LAYS SO MUCH EXPOSED

After Samuel Thompson finally marched away, Jedediah Preble breathed a sigh of relief. Preble knew that if Thompson had succeeded in his "defense" of Falmouth, it would have meant the destruction of the whole town.

The chain of events that had led to Thompson's arrival had been rapid and unprecedented. It had started when a Tory, Captain Coulson, had tried to import rigging and sails for a ship that he was building in the harbor at Falmouth's Casco Neck that spring. The provincial government was not allowing any imports from England; Coulson knew this, but he was under contract with the Royal Navy and he was determined to rig his ship. The local committee of inspection ordered Coulson to send the cargo back to England, so he enlisted the help of Captain Mowatt of His Majesty's Royal Navy, who sailed into the rocky harbor in his sloop of war, the *Canceau*, in early April 1775.

While Mowatt's presence irritated the merchants of the Neck, he had not caused any alarm among them. Preble described him as "a gentleman." When conversation turned to Mowatt, Preble pointed out that his "conduct since he has been here has given no grounds of suspicion he has any design to distress or injure us." In fact, he had actually been quite helpful, Preble pointed out to his friends. "He has afforded his assistance to sundry vessels in distress."

However, the presence of a Royal Navy sloop in the harbor took on a whole new meaning on April 21 when the latest news from Boston reached the Neck. The Massachusetts militia had engaged the British troops in battle. The fighting had begun. Two more Royal Navy boats joined Mowatt in the harbor a couple of days later, and the townspeople were concerned. As news carried from the Neck to outlying areas, facts turned into rumors and concern grew into alarm.

At the end of April, in nearby Brunswick, Samuel Thompson reported to the Provincial Congress that he had seized a Tory ship in his harbor and confiscated two hundred white pine masts. He also made mention of "cruel murders" that the British had committed in the province of Maine. He must have been referring to some false news, but he was incensed by the rumor. "Finding that the sword is drawn first on their side," he said, "we shall be animated with that noble Spirit that wise men ought to be until our Just Rights and Liberties are secured to us."

Back on the Neck, with Mowatt still anchored in sight, Preble received news that Thompson intended to sail into Falmouth Harbor and take the *Canceau* by force. Falmouth's Committee of Correspondence promptly wrote to tell him that the members thought the plan was ill-advised, "as it would throw this town into the greatest confusion imaginable."

Thompson replied that he would drop the plan, so it came as a total shock to the committee members when they heard that Thompson had landed secretly, under protection of pine trees on Back Cove, with sixty of his townsmen. Then, as luck would have it, or rather ill luck, Thompson came upon the *Canceau*'s physician, the Neck's Episcopal minister John Wiswall and Captain Mowatt himself walking on Munjoy's Hill. Thompson was soon holding the three captive at Marston's Tavern.

The village was in chaos, with Thompson's rowdy troops holding sway with their prisoners at the local tavern, the officer in command on board the ship threatening to fire on the town and the townspeople in a panic.

The senior officer on board the *Canceau* was frantic to get his commanding officer back and boldly announced that the rebels had until evening to conduct Mowatt's safe return or he would set his cannons on them. He fired twice to show that he meant business, and even though there was no shot in the cannons, the people in the village responded in alarm. "It frightened the women and children to such a degree," reported Preble, "that some crawled under wharves, some ran down cellar, and some out of town." Preble was not a man to exaggerate, but he was quick to add that "such a shocking scene was never presented to view here."

Preble and the other civic leaders were as upset as anyone in the provinces concerning British trade practices, and they were by no means Tory

"Town Meeting, October, 1775." From *Centennial Celebration*.

sympathizers. They were, however, far more eager to keep the peace in their community than were Thompson and his gang. They did not call the Neck home. In an effort to ease tensions, Preble and Enoch Freeman, another leading citizen, offered themselves to Thompson as hostages in return for Mowatt, his doctor and Wiswall, with the understanding that Mowatt was on parole from Thompson and would return from his ship the next morning.

Preble was alarmed when he woke at daybreak to find the town flooded with militia from surrounding towns. Word had spread to Gorham, Scarborough, Cape Elizabeth and Stroudwater, and there were minutemen, nearly six hundred of them, ready for a fight, ready for civil war to begin there and then. When it became clear that Mowatt was not going to return to land to honor his parole, the armed men became furious and took their frustration out on Preble and Freeman by keeping them confined and not allowing them any dinner or contact with their families. Mowatt wrote to Preble, explaining that one of his men on shore had reported that Thompson's men were planning to kill Mowatt the minute he stepped on land and that this was why he hadn't honored his pledge. Preble and Freeman were eventually released on the promise to provide food to the growing mob. When they did, Thompson complained that it wasn't enough. He also demanded money from the town coffers for his "time and expense," a payment town authorities weren't about to make.

Tensions were running as high between the people on the Neck and the mob from the surrounding towns as they were between the British and the Mainers. The ruffians, under the quasi-sanction of the provincial government, set up an inquisition of known Tories and raided their houses. From Sheriff Tyng's they stole a silver cup and tankard and a gold-laced hat. They used Coulson's house as a barrack and drank the liquor in his cellar.

The disturbances continued for days. While minutemen in Concord and Lexington gathered their dead and nursed their wounds, the ruffians on the coast of Maine were doing their best to provoke the British navy. Drunk on stolen rum, they fired a musket at Mowatt's ship, damaging the side; they seized Coulson's boat and dragged it through the streets.

The situation escalated when Mowatt sent word that he would fire on the town in retaliation. Exasperated, Preble and his fellow town leaders replied that they were not at fault and had no control over the mob. Mowatt continued to insist that if as much as one more shot were fired on his ship, he would consider the town in an open state of rebellion and set his cannon sights on it.

Finally, the chaos subsided. Tired from days of wreaking havoc on the village, many of the ruffians began to see the folly in provoking Mowatt into firing on the town. Gradually they realized that they should be at home, caring for their loved ones or preparing for deployment by the provisional government of Massachusetts rather than playing vigilante in someone else's local dispute. The troops began to disperse. When all of the rabble-rousers were gone, Mowatt sailed out of Falmouth Harbor, and the residents of the Neck breathed a sigh of relief.

"Colonel Thompson, we doubt not, is a true friend to his country, and a man of courage and resolution," Preble said charitably, "but as our town lays so much exposed to the Navy, that had he succeeded in his attempt…it must have proved the destruction of this town."

Destruction was yet to come.

The Rod of Correction

The cannons' booms sounded like thunder, and the thunder lasted all day. With every cannonball, another piece of Casco Neck shattered. Carcass shells flew from the warships into the wooden buildings and burst into flame. Musket balls took out windows and steeples; grapeshot sprayed into houses and barns. The screams of the townspeople mingled with the explosive sound of destruction. On a warship in the harbor, behind the smoke and the cannons, Lieutenant Henry Mowatt viewed the chaos. He had his orders; the punishment was just.

Since Mowatt's last visit in April, the people of Falmouth had continued their rebellion against England's king and Parliament. About one month after the Loyalist Captain Coulson had caused trouble by calling Mowatt to aid in his efforts to rig a ship for the Royal Navy, Coulson had the nerve to sail into the harbor to pick up a cargo of masts. He was not welcomed back. Townspeople put his masts and timber in the river and floated them upstream. They were not about to let the troublemaking Tory leave town with goods for His Majesty's Royal Navy ever again. In July, Falmouth sent two companies of about sixty men each to Cambridge to join the Continental army. The people of Falmouth were solidly on the side of the rebels in the conflict.

When Mowatt's *Canceau* and three other ships sailed into the harbor in October 1775, they assumed that he was there to forage for supplies. The next day, townspeople on shore watched with mounting fear as the ships lined up in an attack formation before the town. When Mowatt sent a messenger to shore, they watched the progress of his rowboat with every stroke and followed behind him as he took his message to town hall, where it was read aloud.

Mowatt began by charging the townspeople with "premeditated attacks on the prerogatives of the best of sovereigns." He then scolded them as if they were naughty children taunting a patient father. Time after time they had "experienced…Britain's long forbearance of the Rod of Correction, and the merciful and paternal extension of her hands to embrace you." Mowatt sounded personally hurt as he continued: "And in place of a dutiful and grateful return to your King and Parent state, you have been guilty of the most unpardonable rebellion." His orders were to "execute a just Punishment on the Town of Falmouth," and he warned them to "remove without delay the Human Species out of the said town." He gave them two hours.

The reading of the letter ended, and no one spoke a word. Their fatherland had unquestionably become the enemy. As the reality of the situation began to set in, the townspeople's first response was to try to negotiate. They appointed Jedediah Preble and two other town leaders to try and reason with Mowatt. Preble and the others rowed out to the *Canceau* and were allowed to go aboard. They tried to talk Mowatt out of the attack.

Impossible, he said. He had his orders. In fact, he wasn't even authorized to give them the warning he had issued. Preble was persuasive, and after much discussion, he convinced Mowatt to postpone firing on the town until

"The Mowatt Conference" (1775). From *Centennial Celebration.*

eight o'clock the next morning. Before then, Mowatt wanted them to turn over all their cannons, arms and ammunition.

Preble and the committee weren't sure that the townspeople would agree to this, but they took the terms back to the meetinghouse for a decision. Mowatt would have his answer in the morning, but meanwhile townsmen were in agreement. They would not hand over their arms and render themselves defenseless in a time of war. If that meant taking a few cannon blasts, so be it. They had until morning to prepare themselves.

A flurry of activity ensued as residents made arrangements to remove the children and the elderly and frantically packed and transported all of the material goods they could out of town. The next morning, they congregated again in the meetinghouse, where the majority reaffirmed that they would not surrender their weapons. Preble and his delegation met with Mowatt again aboard the *Canceau*, but when the lieutenant saw that no weapons were forthcoming, he gave the men only thirty minutes to get back to shore and find safety.

At 9:30 a.m., "the cannon began to roar with incessant and tremendous fury," Reverend Bailey described later. The bombardment was relentless as the British fired on the town all day. Becoming even more aggressive after the initial assaults, they debarked from their ships and invaded with torches, ordering the inhabitants out and then setting fire to homes and stores. All the boats in the harbor were set aflame and all the wharves torched. Everywhere was chaos. Men were yelling, women screaming, children crying and everyone rushing desperately, trying to save themselves and their possessions from the flames.

Preble's wife, Mehetable, took an axe to the pigpen to free the swine. "It would be a shame to leave the poor dumb creatures to be burnt," she explained to her husband.

On Back Street, Widow Greely refused to leave her tavern. Every time the flames began to encroach on her, she beat them back.

Townspeople fought here and there, one homeowner or another killed a British soldier with musket fire or wounded one with a bayonet, but the civilians were too surprised to mount an organized plan of defense.

The day felt like a nightmare, and the townspeople reacted in shock. The tone of Mowatt's letter might have been one of an angry father, but the relentless bombardment was far more than a slap on the wrist. Mowatt aimed for the all-out destruction of an enemy stronghold.

By evening, the part of Falmouth called the Neck was in ruins. More than four hundred buildings from Fore Street to Back Street had been destroyed. Preble's house and wharf were gone. On Middle Street, the Episcopalian church and the saddle shop were destroyed. On King Street, the apothecary shop and the new courthouse were also gone. Ilsley's Distillery Wharf, Tyng's Wharf and nearly every vessel in the harbor were demolished.

In the field near Jones Lane sat a pile of furniture, paintings, utensils and clothing—a random assortment of goods pulled frantically from houses and carelessly thrown out of the way of the flames.

When the townspeople attempted to note the casualties of the day, they realized that no one had died in the fire or been killed by the enemy, although several of the British had been killed. Tories claimed later that Mowatt had tears in his eyes when he gave the order to fire. He must have held a tight grip on his men to ensure that none of them carelessly or ruthlessly took the lives of any townspeople. Mowatt had punished the errant children of the British Crown by destroying their property but had spared their lives.

The prosperous village where cod and lumber and molasses had been traded, where a library and courthouse and churches had been established and where citizens had endeavored to govern themselves in the absence of a ruling class was no more. In its place was a landscape of destruction, charred remnants of a life suddenly gone up in smoke. The townspeople must have realized then, if not before, that what came next would be nothing less than a revolution.

Edward Preble Starts a Navy

Off to Sea

Edward Preble was hard at work hoeing potatoes on his father's farm in Capisic, and he wasn't happy about it. The sixteen-year-old had been stuck on the backwoods farm since leaving Dummer Academy in Massachusetts earlier in the year. He missed his port-side home on Casco Neck. He had been at school when the British destroyed his hometown, and he still couldn't quite believe that his house and his family's wharf were gone. He knew that he should feel lucky that the Preble family owned a farm, a place where they could retreat to and grow food, but he was restless. Tilling a plot of ground in some landlocked field was not for him.

Suddenly, in a fit of temper, Edward threw down the hoe. "By God!" he shouted. "I will do no more of this work!" With that, he began his determined march east. Within a few hours, he could hear the gulls and smell the sea air. A full two years after Mowatt's crushing bombardment, not much had improved at Casco Neck. The few houses that had survived the attack were still surrounded by burned-out shells of buildings, the rubble yet to be cleared. In this time of war and shortages, few had the resources to build anything in their place. The harbor was no longer a thriving merchant port. A few privateers anchored off shore rocked to the gentle waves, and others were moored to makeshift docks. With trade severely restricted by the war, local merchants had refitted their sloops, mounted guns and obtained letters of marque from the provisional government that allowed them to capture enemy merchant ships and confiscate the cargo. To Edward Preble, this sounded like much more fun than hoeing potatoes.

Elizabeth Ross Tyng (circa 1766), wife of Colonel William Tyng. From *Portland in the Past*, by William Goold (1886).

Edward signed on with a privateer and sailed for the West Indies. Life at sea suited him, and within a year, his father had arranged for him to join the Massachusetts's State Marine. In his son, by his second wife, Jedediah saw something of himself. Edward had his height, his quick temper and his preference for action rather than study. He had always wanted to be hunting in the woods or fishing in the bay rather than reading books. Jedediah recalled the time when he had sternly told Edward that he couldn't go on a fishing trip because he hadn't done his chores. Jedediah had been leaving shore when Edward came running, yelling that his chores were finished and insisting that he be allowed to go. When his father still said no, the enraged Edward stood on the shore and threw rocks at his father's boat until Jedediah turned around and went back for him. Now the spirited Edward was old enough for military service, and his energies could be put to good use. As representative to the House of Council, Jedediah was in a position to see that Edward was appointed an officer.

Edward distinguished himself during the War of Independence. He was first lieutenant of the *Winthrop* when it captured a British ship off the coast of Castine. The *Winthrop* pulled alongside the brig at night, and Preble led his men in boarding the enemy vessel. His force was meant to be forty strong, but only fourteen managed to board. Preble's officer hailed him, asking if he needed more men. Knowing that the British could hear their exchange, he called back that he did not. "We have more than we want," he cleverly replied. "We stand in each others' way." Preble's ruse panicked the crew of the brig. Convinced that the enemy had boarded in vast numbers, many were so sure of defeat that they jumped overboard. Boldly entering the officers' cabin, Preble demanded they surrender, which they promptly did. The *Winthrop* had won the brig with virtually no resistance and proudly sailed the prize back to Boston.

When serving aboard the *Protector*, Edward was captured and held on the British prison ship *Jersey*. Conditions were filthy there, the rations were sparse and inmates were often left to die slowly from neglect. Preble, however, was saved by an unlikely ally: Cumberland County's former Royalist sheriff, William Tyng. Preble knew Tyng well from his time on the Neck.

He had heard the story of his father's final run-in with the sheriff in the tense days before Mowatt first sailed his British warship into the harbor. The elder Preble and Tyng had been talking on the street one day about the local rebellion. Tyng was quite sure that he heard Preble say that there would be a mob that night. Moments later, Preble denied saying such a thing.

"You old fool!" Tyng erupted. "I would chastise you worse if you were not an old man!"

"I'll cane you if you say so again!" fired back Preble.

Sheriff Tyng quickly drew his sword. "I'll run you through with this!" he shouted. Undaunted by the sight of Tyng's weapon, Preble grabbed Tyng by the collar and shook him.

The confrontation was drawing a crowd, and apprehension grew. Peacemakers urged the two men to control themselves and finally got them to calm down. Once the anger had subsided, Tyng apologized to Preble. Some townspeople thought that Preble should push the matter further against such a Loyalist bully and assured him that he would have their backing, Preble accepted Tyng's apology. "I desire nothing more," he said.

Four years later, faced with the prospect of doing time on a prison ship, Edward was thankful that his father had acted the gentleman. Tyng had left Falmouth to take refuge in British-occupied New York. He had remained loyal to the Crown, but he had once been a resident of Falmouth, and in

Colonel William Tyng (circa 1790), found in a gold locket. From *Portland in the Past.*

this case, the tie between the two former neighbors proved stronger than the conflict between England and the provinces. Tyng liberated Preble from the prison ship and arranged for him to live ashore while technically still a "prisoner of war."

Back in Falmouth, Edward's father was relieved to hear the good news and immediately contacted Tyng. Despite the two men's sometimes volatile differences, Preble was quick to show his gratitude for the kindness extended to his son. "I have written him my acknowledgements on the subject," he wrote to Edward and added a father's admonition: "Hope your future conduct will be such as to render you in some measure worthy their future notice…Be kind and obliging to all," he continued, no doubt thinking of that day in April when he might have held a grudge but instead was quick to forgive, "for no man ever does a designed injury to another, without doing a greater to himself." Edward's father went on to report news of Mrs. Tyng's mother: "Present your mama's and my best compliments to Colonel Tyng and Lady, and let them know Madam Ross was in good health yesterday." The senior Preble wished his son "a speedy exchange." Under the care of William Tyng, Edward was soon a free man.

After the war, Preble joined the merchant service. He was part owner of several ships and served as the commander of many of them, sailing around the world with whatever cargos would be most profitable. In 1798, he received another navy commission, as first lieutenant on the *Constitution*.

Preble's life at sea had distracted him from finding a wife and starting a family, but now at the age of thirty-eight, he began to think that it was time for marriage. He fell in love with Mary Deering of Portland, which was to be Falmouth's new name. Before he went out to sea for a year, he enlisted the help of Mary's mother in securing her faithfulness. Fearing what might happen while away for so long, Edward stated his case bluntly. "Should Mary Deering bless another with her affections, and not me, I am lost forever," he wrote dramatically. "For heaven's sake, plead for me."

Mary's affections remained fastened to Edward, and two years later, they were married. They were an older couple, possessed of more maturity than most newlyweds. Mary had once been engaged to lawyer who died before they could marry. At thirty-one, she had been single long enough to develop a strong will and a mind of her own, as well as a love of books and solitude. Her broad face was framed by curly light-brown hair, and her slightly slanted blue eyes gave her a calculating look. Edward's thinning hair accentuated his sharp features, and his eyes revealed his intensity. A man of burning drive, Edward had capitalized on his father's wealth and connections and had made his own small fortune in the shipping business. With his marriage into the wealthy Deering family, his future was even more secure.

To most men, marriage in midlife would signal a good time to settle down to a quiet existence. However, the biggest adventure of Edward Preble's eventful life was yet to come.

Fighting the Barbary Pirates

In 1803, residents of Portland read in their local newspaper that Captain Preble had been "appointed to command a squadron now fitting out in the United States for foreign service." In the short news piece, editor Eleazar Jenks explained that the squadron was expected to be composed of seven vessels and would sail in July. Preble's activities were of great interest in his hometown seaport since he was a part of the young country's fledgling navy. Once his secret destination was revealed to be the Barbary Coast, interest grew even stronger. Barbary pirates had been plaguing the growing fleet of merchant ships sailing out of Portland Harbor. Under the rule of the North African pasha, the corsairs were capturing American ships, stealing the cargo and imprisoning entire crews. Capture by a Barbary pirate meant a fate worse than death. They didn't kill their captives or merely imprison them—they turned them into slaves.

Preble's mission was to provide protection for American merchant ships by blockading the port of Tripoli. His official order was to "annoy the enemy" with "all the means in your power." As the *Constitution* sailed for the coast of North Africa, sailors were able to send word home via ships they met in passing, so the *Portland Gazette* was able to report in September that "the officer and crew were in good health." After arriving in the Mediterranean, Preble took on the Moors, calling them a "deep, designing, artful, treacherous set of villains." Preble sent part of his fleet into the harbor in Tangier and told the emperor he was prepared for war. After several days of negotiation, the two sides came to an agreement.

Preble's reputation as a negotiator soared. Back home in Portland, his wife of only two years was somewhat comforted to read Edward's letter: "I have undertaken an arduous task but hope to get honorably through and return to you, never again to separate."

Preble was still protecting American interests in North Africa a few months later when Tripoli captured the USS *Philadelphia* and its crew of

Captain Edward Preble, USN (1761–1807). *U.S. Naval Academy Collection.*

three-hundred. While he couldn't do anything for the prisoners, he was able to set fire to the *Philadelphia* so that it could not be used in the hands of the enemy. The *Portland Gazette* reported that "a letter from Tripoli, Feb. 22, states that the American prisoners had not experienced any severity of treatment in consequence of the destruction of the *Philadelphia* frigate." Preble refused to pay ransom for the prisoners and instead made plans to attack Tripoli to free them. However, he feared that his forces were not strong enough. At the end of May, he wrote to Mary that "I shall be obliged to attack Tripoli under many disadvantages for want of more ships."

Preble and his men made a bold attack on the North African port. They forcefully boarded enemy ships, killed the captains and engaged in hand-to-hand combat with the crew. However, Preble's forces only managed to capture a few small Tripolitan boats. As Preble's efforts toward a clear victory in Tripoli waned, he got news from Washington that he would be replaced by a more senior commanding officer who was already on his way. In his private journal, Preble confessed "how much my feelings are lacerated by this supercedure." Before the new commanding officer arrived, Preble attempted two more attacks on Tripoli, but neither of them did much damage. Preble lost thirteen men when he sent the *Intrepid* into the enemy harbor with orders to ignite the ship and then quickly vacate it, leaving the vessel itself to serve as an exploding weapon that would damage the harbor fortress. However, the *Intrepid* blew up too soon and too far from shore and did little or no damage. In the *Gazette*, the people of Portland read with horror a report from the consul of Algiers describing the attack: "A fire-ship, which was sent forward among the vessels unfortunately took fire before the people on board had cleared themselves, and blew them all into atoms." The attack hit close to home, as the same issue of the paper included an obituary for Portland native Henry Wadsworth: "Off Tripoli, killed by the blowing up of a fire-ship in which he was employed, son of the Honorable Peleg Wadsworth, of this town." Three years later, Henry's sister, Zilpa Wadsworth Longfellow, would name her son after him.

The loss of more men, including a former neighbor from his hometown, dampened Preble's already low spirits. However, he put up a good front for his men, officially telling them that "I could not have been more gratified than by being allowed to command you until the present war was brought to a conclusion, but rank must be attended to."

His officers responded warmly with a written tribute to their commander. "Your supercedure in a command in which you have acquired so much honor to yourself and country is by us deeply regretted," they told him publicly.

The tribute was signed by fifty-three of his officers, many of whom would go on to distinguish themselves in the War of 1812 and would be referred to in the future as "Preble's Boys."

Preble left Tripoli unable to free the American prisoners of war, and an objective observer from the Danish consul dismissed his efforts by saying that "the damage done" was "of absolutely no consequence." Preble might have agreed with that assessment, so he was surprised at the accolades he received when he returned to Washington, D.C. "I cannot but be a little flattered with the reception I have met with here," he wrote to Mary. "The people are disposed to think I have rendered some service to my country."

"Congress is highly impressed with the gallant and meritorious services of Commodore Edward Preble," said General Jackson in a resolution read before the U.S. Senate. Political leaders still forming the foundations of their new military were grateful for a national hero. The Senate resolution proclaimed that through Preble and his crew's efforts "the naval character of the American nation and people has in the infancy of their national existence acquired a respect and rank among the nations of the earth highly honorable and exalted." The resolution called for commemorative gold medals to be struck and a bonus of one month's pay to be given to the crew.

Preble was finally ready for a quieter, more stationary life. While in Washington, D.C., he agreed to be the contractor for four new boats for the U.S. Navy. The boats could be built in Portland and Newburyport, which meant that Preble could return to his hometown, to his wife and to friends and family. By June 1805, he had boat builders in Portland working on vessels of his own design, and Mary was pregnant with their first child. Preble proved to be a tough contractor, determined to get the lowest price and vigilant in supervising every step of the work. A part of each day was now spent on the familiar wharves and shipyards he had known as a young boy. He also took time for other pursuits he had enjoyed in his youth, like hunting, fishing and making apple cider. Preble hoped for a son, telling a friend that "I wish with you that the child may be a boy and that he may live to be useful to his country. Indeed, I think males are generally better calculated to make their way good through this rough world than the other sex." Preble got his wish when Mary gave birth in February. The couple named their son Edward Deering. Preble was a loving father and looked forward to seeing his son laid next to him in bed in the morning "smiling and innocent as an angel."

He was proud of his ships, too, as he sent them out into the world. He proclaimed his first bomb ketch, the *Etna*, to be "as well-built and as handsome a vessel of her size as ever floated." The U.S. Navy was also happy with the vessels and contracted with Preble to build eight more. Times were good and prosperous for the Prebles, and they began to make plans to build a new three-story mansion on Congress Street.

Unfortunately, Preble's years of domestic happiness with Mary and his son in the town of his youth were short-lived. Stomach ailments that had plagued him most of his life grew worse, and in June 1807, he was so sick that he couldn't leave his room. In the nursery little Edward played with his toys, on Congress Street workmen laid the foundation for his new mansion and in the shipyard builders worked on his plans for new gunboats. But Edward Preble was forced to take to his bed as the activity buzzed around him. A few times that summer, he roused himself to go out to sea on one of the gunboats, and sometimes the sea air would revive him for a while, but his illness never left him that summer. Tensions were building with Britain, and the navy was pressuring Preble to produce gunboats quickly. Meanwhile, Portland's economy was faltering due to trade embargos, and the new home-building project was taxing the family resources. Preble's condition worsened as the summer went on. By August, he was never well enough to leave his room. At the end of August, he died at home at the age of forty-six.

Preble passed away in the afternoon, and that evening many of Portland's leading citizens gathered to plan his funeral. They endeavored to "make arrangements for entombing his remains with every possible mark of respect."

The *Eastern Argus* lauded its native son as "hospitable, generous, philanthropic and amiable." The editor singled out Preble's actions on the Barbary Coast for special merit on the day of his funeral: "The citizens of the United States, to the latest posterity, will never cease to venerate and applaud his gallant conduct in the bombardment and attack of Tripoli." Preble might have thought that his hometown paper exaggerated his success in Tripoli when it wrote that "never were greater abilities as a tactician more honorably depictured than in that bold and decisive enterprise."

All the bells in town tolled for one hour the morning of his funeral, and flags flew at half-mast from every ship in the harbor. At one o'clock in the afternoon, every store and office closed its door for the day. The funeral procession began at Preble's house, where Reverend Deane said prayers, the Masons performed their rites and musicians played a dirge. Led by local military companies, Masonic officers and town officials, Preble's funeral procession wound through town. Following the casket was his family and, behind them, the rest of the mourners. Soldiers fired their guns every minute, punctuating the mourner's steps.

Early Entertainment

The Pig of Knowledge

All kinds of entertainment found its way to Portland in the summer, even in 1798. That July, townspeople were buzzing about the latest attraction to appear in the Assembly Room on King Street. The Pig of Knowledge was advertised in the *Portland Gazette* to be "the wonder of all Europe." Eager patrons bought tickets in advance at Captain Davis's Tavern on Free Street and laughed at the idea that a pig could perform all the amazing feats promised: "He reads print or writing, spells, tells the time of day, both the hours and minutes…distinguishes colors…and will answer any question in the four first rules of arithmetic," the promoter promised.

Portlanders had been hearing about amazing pigs for a while. News had reached them from England about extraordinary feats performed by swine. Someone said that they had read about such a pig in James Boswell's *Life of Samuel Johnson*, and someone else said they had seen a cartoon of a learned pig in a London newspaper.

The Pig of Knowledge captivated the Portland audience, as it had others on the East Coast. After the performance, many agreed that the pig was "far the greatest curiosity ever exhibited on the continent of America."

"How could it be?" they wondered. "How could it read and tell time?"

Some speculated that the beast was a man reincarnate, but that idea was quickly shot down by the conservative Puritans. The trainer had made a deal with the devil, they explained, and the performance had been sinful. Others thought that the pig's tricks could be taught if the trainer were a tyrant. The

Samuel Smith (1702–1795). From *Journals of the Reverend Thomas Smith and the Reverend Samuel Deane: Pastors of the First Church in Portland* (1849).

pig must have been abused and tortured to get such a performance out of it, they said.

A few years later, a book came out in Boston that answered the audience's speculation. In *The Expositor; or Many Mysteries Unravelled*, trainer William Pinchbeck explained his methods. His pig's talent did not lie in learning to read letters in print, he explained, but in reading his trainer. The pig would learn to pick the correct letter by listening to the trainer, who would "snuff," or breathe through his nose, when the animal came to the card with the correct letter on it. More surprisingly, Pinchbeck contended, the blatant signals become unnecessary, "for the animal is so sagacious, that he will appear to read your thoughts. The position you stand in, not meaning any stipulated place, or certain gestures, but what will naturally arise from your anxiety, will determine the card to your pupil."

"Carrying the Mail" (circa 1786). From *Centennial Celebration*.

The secret of the Pig of Knowledge was in the extraordinary relationship between pig and trainer. "You are not to beat him into the knowledge of your design," Pinchbeck explained, "but to coax him to it, if possible."

Pinchbeck's show was successful because it truly was extraordinary, he said. "I have been as much amazed at the performances of this animal as the spectators before whom I exhibited him."

The Evils of Theater

In 1805, the curtain closed on Portland's last theatrical performance for more than a decade. The stage went dark at Union Hall on Free Street because theater itself was declared evil.

Theater had flourished in Portland ever since Snelling Powell had arrived in the growing city in 1794. By then, more than two thousand people lived in Portland, and the booming shipping business allowed for a class of people with money, leisure time and an appreciation for lively entertainment. Powell's company arrived out of Boston full of enterprise and energy, as well as at least a little talent. Its first production offered patrons two plays, a comedy called *Lyar* and a farce called *Modern Antiques or the Merry Mourners.* Powell himself was one of the leading characters, and his wife played a role as well. Powell was the driving force and the business mind behind the company, but he had a valuable asset in his wife, Elizabeth, an actress of true ability. The Powells continued to travel from their home base of Boston every summer to stage plays in Portland, and their performances were well attended.

Every July, a notice in the *Portland Gazette* would announce the arrival of the company and the expectation that its run would be "superior to any before in this town."

"S. Powell is contemptible as a player (and I believe as a man)," eighteen-year-old Eliza Southgate told her cousin in 1801. "He puffs and blows so incessantly that it is enough to put one into a fever to see him…he cannot gradually bring his passion to the height, but he thunders it out without any preparation, and the unvarying monotony of his voice is truly disgusting."

And yet Eliza was a fan of theater and found Elizabeth Harrison Powell to be the company's saving grace. "How I admire that woman!" she continued. "She is perfectly at home on the stage, and yet there is no levity in her appearance; she has great energy, acts with spirit, with feeling, yet never rants."

An evening's entertainment usually included two plays; in 1802, the company performed both a comedy (*Poverty and Honour or the Sighs of a Daughter*) and a comic opera. Tickets for the show were fifty cents for the pit and seventy-five cents for the boxes. *Portland Gazette* editor Eleazar Jenks noted that the first week of performances drew large crowds; however, one night the play was disrupted by "the intrusion of some turbulent fellows." Evidently, Powell increased security after the incident because Jenks reported that "we are requested to assure the public that measures have been taken by the proprietors and manager to avoid a repetition of such unjustifiable conduct." Unfortunately, disruptions by "turbulent fellows," probably young and drunk, seemed to be a fairly frequent occurrence at the theater. As a result, the more conservative, puritanical residents began to grumble.

In 1804, the company closed out the season in September with what must have been a long night of entertainment for both audience and performers. They began with Shakespeare's *Richard III*, followed that with a ballet in pantomime and then finished the performance with a comic opera.

In 1805, the Powells returned as usual. Well established now in Portland, they were happier than ever to be back. At the beginning of the season, they never imagined that it would be their last. Editor Jenks was enthusiastic, as usual, about the summer entertainment: "The Theatre, of this town, we are happy to observe, has received some valuable reinforcements." *The Castle Spectre*

Portrait of Elizabeth Arnold Poe (1796), mother of Edgar Allan Poe and actress on the Portland stage. From *Music and Musicians of Maine*, by George Thorton Edwards.

had been popular, he said, with "a crowded and respectable audience." Jenks had great praise for Elizabeth Powell, who "if possible, still more endeared herself to those who have ever admired her performances." Mr. Fox and Mr. Usher "exhibited marks of great improvement," he said diplomatically. Jenks was probably a genuine fan of theater, but he was also, no doubt, a fan of the advertising revenue the company provided for his paper.

As that summer went on, the grumblings about the theater grew louder, and Jenks's praise became more frequent. To counter claims that the theater attracted a rough and boisterous crowd, Jenks noted with every review that the productions performed in front of a "respectable" audience.

Complaints aside, Powell's theater company was a well-established success in Portland. Due to the company's standing, Snelling Powell might have miscalculated how much conservative resistance he would face when he announced plans to erect a building devoted entirely to theatrical productions. This idea flew in the face of Puritan convictions for a good number of Portland residents, the majority of whose heritage was with the Plymouth Colony. Theater had traditionally been considered sinful in their world, and old notions were hard to change.

Jenks reported receiving lots of letters at the *Gazette* regarding the theater issue and published two in September that he said "embrace the principal ideas of the others." The first one came from someone who signed his letter "One of Many." He urged all to attend the meeting regarding the proposal so that "by his attendance and rational conduct, he may save from dissipation, or ruin, his child, his relation, or acquaintance." The anti-theater contingent came at the issue from a practical standpoint. The problem with the theater, according to "One of Many," was that it would be a fire hazard. Constructing a large wooden building three stories high and in a section of town where water was already in short supply would be too dangerous. He appealed to some of Portland's worst memories. The bombardment and the burning of the town by the British at the onset of the Revolution had occurred just thirty years before. The writer reminded Portlanders that their town had "already once been reduced to ashes." He concluded with one more warning about the building: "No one who has any reputation to lose… will favor or promote its completion."

"The stage, well-conducted, has uniformly been viewed, in all civilized and polite communities, not only as the source of rational amusement, but also as the friend to virtue and morals," countered the other writer, who did not sign his name and evidently didn't count the Puritans as members of "civilized and polite communities." He went on to acknowledge that despite the great work of the past by playwrights like William Shakespeare, the stage had "depreciated much of late." He voiced the fears of the opposition—that with a theater in town "the temptation will be too great, everyone is to run theatre-mad, and the ruin of morals and property is to follow." But this is foolish, he said. The people of Portland have "prudence and discretion" and are capable of governing themselves.

At the subsequent town meeting, three men led the debate about the theater. At the town hall, those present would have been dressed in the fashion of the day: breeches fastened at the knee over long stockings, a dark waistcoat, high collar and ruffled shirt, long hair pulled back in a ponytail.

Thomas Wait spoke in favor of the theater. Wait was not a Puritan but an Episcopalian, former Royalist and member of the Church of England who had managed to keep a low profile during the Revolution. Wait had been in trouble with the law in Falmouth as a young man (he had been indicted for dancing). Now he spoke in favor of another pleasure that would be denied to him by the Puritan majority.

Woodbury Storer spoke in opposition to the theater. Storer had been baptized in Falmouth's First Parish in 1776. The First Parish had been the first church in what was now called Portland, and its roots were unquestionably with the Puritans of Plymouth Colony. Storer was a successful merchant, and as a senator representing Cumberland County in the Massachusetts legislature, he could wield a lot of influence.

The other Portlander who spoke in opposition to the theater was Samuel Freeman (Deacon Freeman) of the First Parish Church. An active Patriot during the Revolution, he had become a successful merchant, selectman and judge of probate.

In democratic town meeting fashion, a vote was taken after the debate. The interests of live performance, of the Powells and of theater in general, were defeated. Voters passed a resolution against the theater building that stated that "the evils arising from a frequent attendance at the theatre, or play house, are greater than any advantage that can be derived therefrom." A theater would "in no way promote the interest of religion…but…may and probably will have a contrary tendency." In addition to defeating Powell's theater proposal, townspeople called for the selectmen to appeal to the legislature to establish a law prohibiting all theatrical performances. Two of the biggest opponents of theater were a selectman and a legislator, and the appeal was made with conviction.

The following March, a brief notice appeared in the *Gazette*: "We understand the Legislature of the state have passed a law, prohibiting all theatrical exhibitions within this Commonwealth, unless leave is previously obtained from the Court of Sessions for the County where the performances are to take place."

Theater was outlawed. An economic depression descended on Portland the next year, and then the War of 1812 unfolded. Residents were preoccupied with more serious concerns and didn't have the time or money for theater, even if it had been legal. The Powells retreated to Boston; the stage went dark and it remained dark until the next generation brought it back to light once again.

The Hanging of Joseph Drew

Joseph Drew was taken from his Portland jail cell dressed in a white robe and cap, with a halter around his neck. As he walked out of the prison yard, the first things he saw were the high sheriff, the deputies and his own coffin.

"Life is sweet!" he cried between sobs. "Life is sweet!"

Six months before, in December 1807, Deputy Sheriff Ebenezer Parker had arrested Drew's friend, Levi Quimby, in Saccarappa, just west of Portland. The region was in the throes of a depression; Quimby's crime was that he couldn't pay his debts. A lot of people, both rich and poor, couldn't pay their debts in 1807, and as a result some paid the price in debtors prison.

In January, Quimby managed to escape from Parker's custody. Armed with a club, he fled to his friend Joseph Drew's blacksmith shop and locked the door behind him. Parker pursued him and yelled through the door that he must be allowed to enter and seize his prisoner. Drew and Quimby yelled threats at Parker in return. Parker's anger was growing as he tried harder and harder to break down the door. When he finally succeeded, he was met with Drew and Quimby, whose rage matched his own. A hot nail rod whizzed by his head, and then he ducked to avoid a sledge. Parker looked around frantically for Quimby but couldn't see him. Suddenly, Quimby emerged from a dark corner and threw his club to Drew, who then swung it at Parker's head. Parker lunged for Drew, and Drew swung again. As Parker fell to the ground, Drew shut the door on him and fastened his windows.

Cumberland County Courthouse, 1785. *Courtesy of the Portland Public Library Special Collections and Archives.*

"They can send as many sheriffs as they please. We'll serve them all like we did this one!" Drew told Quimby triumphantly.

Drew might not have boasted so proudly if he had known how much damage he had done. A week later, Parker died from his blows to the head, leaving his illiterate wife and children behind. Joseph Drew was indicted for murder.

In May, a jury returned the verdict of guilty, and the death sentence was pronounced. Afterward, many of Portland's ministers made the trip to the jailhouse to visit Drew. He told them all that he was angry about the verdict and hopeful for a pardon. He never seemed to repent, until it became clear that no pardon would come his way.

The day before his hanging, he signed a document called "A Sketch of the Life and Confession of Joseph Drew." It was "drawn up at my request and as expressive of my present frame of mind." However, the language used sounded very similar to that of Reverend Kellogg in the sermon he gave the next day. In the document, Drew described the trial as "impartial" and claimed that "the Spirit of Christ has taken from me the heart of enmity and of a murderer and given me the heart of a penitent and made me willing

"The Way Ye Folk Went to Meeting" (circa 1786). From *Centennial Celebration*.

to renounce all my sins…and to receive the Lord Jesus as my only and sufficient Savior." After the execution, when the document was printed in the local paper, some skeptics questioned whether these were Drew's sincere sentiments or simply Kellogg's invention.

On the day of his hanging, Drew walked to Munjoy Hill between two clergymen. He ascended the ladder to the gallows with composure, while below him a large and curious crowd surrounded his coffin. The high sheriff read his death warrant and asked Drew if he had anything to say. He did not.

Reverend Kellogg's sermon seemed aimed at the young boys in the crowd. "Few men in their first steps of unrighteousness venture upon gross immoralities and enormous acts of violence," he told the crowd. "But from carelessness and want of serious consideration, and from neglect of religion, in connection with the natural progress of their corrupt dispositions, they fall by indefensible degrees into the madness of iniquity."

As Kellogg delivered his sermon, Drew stood silently, his eyes shaded by his cap, his mouth moving noiselessly but continually, as if in prayer.

Kellogg completed his sermon.

The plank was let go, and Drew dropped to his death.

The crowd said not a word.

The Vanquished Enemy and the Dying Conqueror

I remember the sea-fight far away,
How it thundered o'er the tide!
And the dead captains as they lay
In their graves, o'erlooking the tranquil bay
Where they in battle died.
–Henry Wadsworth Longfellow, "My Lost Youth"

On a crisp September morning in 1813, news traveled quickly from the observatory on Munjoy Hill to the shops on Fore Street and the wharves in Portland Harbor. The *Enterprise* and the *Boxer* had been identified coming into port, with the American colors flying over the latter, a British ship. Portlanders left their apothecary shops and millineries, left off hauling their casks of molasses and carts of lumber, to watch eagerly as the United States *Enterprise* sailed into view with its prize: His Majesty's brig, the *Boxer*. With the young United States at war with England again, the naval victory was heartening news to those on shore, and they were eager to hear the details firsthand.

It had been a "brilliant affair," the *Eastern Argus* reported. In fact, it had demonstrated American dominance over England. The victory had "placed at a still greater distance all doubt of the decided superiority of our naval heroes."

The resting place of Samuel Blyth (died 1813), Eastern Cemetery, Portland, Maine. *Photo by Kate Johnson.*

The story of the battle circulated quickly throughout the town. When Lieutenant William Burrows had come upon the *Boxer* at sea near Pemaquid, he had been eager to engage it in battle. However, the fighting had barely begun when the twenty-eight-year-old was struck and seriously wounded. "At twenty minutes past three our brave commander fell," one of the officers on board explained, "and while lying on deck, refusing to be carried below, raised his head and requested that the flag might never be struck."

Burrows lived long enough to know that his request was realized. After he was struck, Lieutenant Edward McCall became the commanding officer. He oversaw a battle that lasted only about forty-five minutes. The *Enterprise* managed to outmaneuver the *Boxer* and make solid hits to the port bow and topmast before the British vessel surrendered. When McCall took prisoner the sixty-four British soldiers, he learned that their commander, thirty-year-old Samuel Blyth, had been killed in the initial fusillade. The battle had lasted less than an hour and had not been especially deadly. And yet one commanding officer had been killed and the other seriously wounded.

Following custom, the officers took Blyth's sword and presented it to Burrows. "When the sword of the vanquished enemy was presented to the dying conqueror, he clasped his hands and said, 'I am satisfied; I die

The *Boxer* (1813). From *Portland in the Past.*

contented,' nor till then, would he consent to be carried below," recalled an officer as he related the battle to the curious on shore. Burrows died later that night.

Shortly after the *Boxer* surrendered, the Americans threw overboard the bodies of the twenty British sailors who had been killed. The following morning, the *Enterprise* flag was slowly lowered to half-mast, with the crew assembled. McCall read the burial service for the two American sailors who had been killed in the battle; their bodies were also committed to the sea. The only bodies that remained to take back to port were those of the commanders.

After McCall sailed proudly into Portland Harbor, he anchored the boats just above Union Wharf, and the prisoners were removed to Fort Scammel. Local doctors and volunteers took the wounded; both British and Americans labored through the day and the next night nursing the injuries.

Portlanders learned that the *Boxer* had lost its doctor when it needed him most. British sailors told of how they had been hailed by a fishing boat off Monehegan Island before sighting the *Enterprise*. The fishermen asked if the ship's doctor might go ashore to tend a crippled islander. Captain Blyth had generously allowed his doctor to leave the ship to treat the American civilian. It was shortly after the doctor left in the fishing boat that the battle had begun, so the British sailors had been without a doctor on board to care for their wounds.

But that wasn't the strangest story told about Blyth and the *Boxer*. Slowly, rumors began to spread along the wharves and into town about a deal that had been struck. A much-needed shipment of woolen goods for the U.S. military had arrived in Bath on the *Margaretta.* The brig had been chartered by Portland merchant Charles Tappan out of British New Brunswick. Some said that they had heard on good authority that Blyth had used the *Boxer* to convoy the *Margaretta* from New Brunswick as far as Bath. In fact, when the ships had hit thick fog off Quoddy Head, the *Boxer* had taken the *Margaretta* in tow so they would not get separated.

Why would Blyth do such thing? If one looked in the pocket of the jacket still worn by the dead commander, he would have found a one-hundred-pound bill of exchange—some whispered it was a gift from Tappan for taking care of the *Margaretta.*

No, said others. The bill of exchange had been replaced with money that couldn't be traced. Tappan wanted no suspicion raised when British naval officials went through the captain's belongings.

The resting place of Captain William Burrows (died 1813), Eastern Cemetery, Portland, Maine. *Photograph by Kate Johnson.*

Speculation about Blyth's role in convoying a cargo of American military supplies never became public. Soon the plans for his funeral were announced in the *Argus*: "The remains of the intrepid and gallant William Burrows, late commander of the United State brig *Enterprise*, and his brave competitor Samuel Blyth, late commander of the British brig *Boxer*, will be entombed in this town today with military and civic honors." The *Argus* touted the "humanity to the vanquished enemy" shown by the American officers and crew. Portlanders decided to follow their lead. Despite America's war with England, the people of Portland honored Captain Blyth of the English navy with fanfare equal to that of their American commander.

Two days after the remains had arrived in Portland Harbor, townspeople organized a double funeral that attracted a large crowd from not only Portland but also the surrounding area. Mourners along Fore Street watched as shipmates from each vessel rowed the coffins to shore, and guns from each ship fired alternately at one-minute intervals. The rowers stroked the water at each blast. The Portland Rifle Company and two infantry companies waited for the coffins on shore and escorted them along Fore Street to Pleasant, High, Main and Middle Streets. The procession stopped at the Second Parish Church for solemn music and the rites of sepulcher and then proceeded up Munjoy Hill to the burial ground. The elderly watched with their memories of the War for Independence still fresh in mind; young men watched with impatience to find adventure for themselves; and the very young watched in awe as the procession marched through town.

City officials and clergy followed behind the military escort, the officers of each ship served as pallbearers and the crews followed behind the caskets. The collector of the port and other United States government officials took up the rear. At Eastern Cemetery, the committal prayers were said as the bodies were lowered into the ground and the bugle played taps for the American and "Last Post" for the Englishman. Burrows was from Philadelphia and Blyth from Portsea in England, so both commanders died far from home with no family members present at their last rites. However, Portlanders provided them with all the tribute they could.

Two years later, a third sailor was buried next to Burrows and Blyth on Munjoy Hill. In the battle between the *Boxer* and the *Enterprise*, midshipman Kervin Waters had survived a direct hit but had been seriously wounded. When the *Enterprise* sailed out of Portland Harbor later that fall, Waters was still not well enough to go with them, nor was he well enough to travel back to his home in Washington, D.C. The sixteen-year-old boy was forced to find lodgings in Portland and boarded in a private home on King Street.

He was well enough sometimes to get out of doors for a walk. His friendly manner endeared him to the townspeople, and his stories of the battle and his other adventures at sea captivated the young boys in the neighborhood. Waters's condition declined, and after two years he passed away at the age of eighteen. Townspeople buried the midshipman in a place of honor next to his commanding officer. By then, the war was over, never to be forgotten by the boys who had watched the *Enterprise* triumphantly sail into harbor with its British prize. A monument was erected for Waters with a plaque that read: "The young men of Portland erect this stone as testimony of their respect for his valor and virtues."

The Plains Tinware Colony

In the 1830s, Stevens Plains bustled with activity. Tinsmiths, some of the best in their craft, created elaborate trays and breadbaskets. Their assistants painted them with brightly colored flowers, and expert japanners lacquered them for a shiny finish. Many more tinsmiths kept busy making basins, dippers, colanders and various kinds of kitchenware from tin plate. Other craftsmen worked in pewter or the less expensive Britannia ware, creating teapots, coffee urns and lamps. Some entrepreneurs turned their expertise into making stovepipes. Comb makers made hair ornaments from tortoiseshell and horn.

There was always a constant stream of peddlers coming and going from Stevens Plains with their tin carts brimming with these specialty wares. They were ready to sell and barter throughout New England and even into Quebec and Nova Scotia. The neighborhood general store, stocked with items received in trade, attracted shoppers from all over the Casco Bay area.

The bustling Plains Tinware Colony began with one tinsmith, Zachariah Brackett Stevens. He could trace his roots back to Anthony Brackett, who had established the Brackett farm on Falmouth Neck, and even further back to George Cleeve, the area's very first white settler. Stevens's grandfather, Zachariah Brackett, had been too tough to give up on the area, even after watching his father and half-brother die in the Indian wars.

Stevens grew up in Falmouth and learned the blacksmith trade, as well as some of the rudimentary skills of tinsmithing, from his grandfather. When he was still a young man, he went to Boston to apprentice, probably with Paul Revere. There he learned the English style of tinsmithing and developed

Samuel Deane (1733–1814). From *Portland, ME. First Parish Church: 75th Anniversary*.

skill in making decorative, sophisticated pieces that most rural artisans could not make. He returned to the Portland area a expert craftsman and set up his business in about 1800. A few years later, he was joined by Thomas Brisco, who brought new skills to the neighborhood. Brisco had run a japanning, or liquid varnish, factory owned by Paul Revere. He had married Revere's niece, Sarah Rose, and they had moved to Stevens Plains with Sarah's five nieces, the Francis sisters. The fledgling tinware colony was lucky to have them. All talented artists, the girls painted much of the tinware in colorful flowers of red and yellow. Sally Francis was the best artist of all and eventually married Zachariah's son, Samuel. After her marriage, she turned her attention to her home, where she painted every available surface with roses.

During the 1820s, demand for Plains Colony items rapidly grew. Zachariah built a new general store and a new shop and hired more workers.

He and Brisco built up the peddler trade, which attracted more and more craftsmen. The neighborhood also included a Universalist church, of which Zachariah and many of his neighbors were members. They worked together, worshiped together and intermarried. Tinsmith Walter Goodrich married Maria, another of the Francis sisters. Pewterer Rufus Dunham married Emmeline, one of Zachariah's daughters. Zachariah's son, Alfred, married Oliver Buckley's daughter…and so it went, a tightknit community dedicated to craftsmanship and trade.

Stevens Plains was called Steven's Avenue by 1842, when fire broke out in Zachariah's blacksmith shop and burned out of control, destroying his tin shop and the shop belonging to his son-in-law, Rufus Dunham. Life on Steven's Avenue was never the same after the fire. With the advent of the factory and the railroad, the craftsman's and the peddler's roles were declining and the colony never recovered. As sixty-four-year-old Zachariah surveyed the destruction of his tinsmith shop and the lifestyle that went with it, he must have known that the fire signaled the end of an era. He might have despaired that his work would be forgotten.

He never could have imagined that more than one hundred years later, his wares would be sought by collectors all over the world and sell for thousands of dollars.

Privateering, Rum Drinking and the Customs Collector

I remember the black wharves and the slips,
And the sea tides tossing free;
And the Spanish sailors with bearded lips,
And the beauty and mystery of the ships,
And the magic of the sea.
–*Henry Wadsworth Longfellow, "My Lost Youth"*

The *Fox* Gets a Prize

Trade was slow during the War for Independence, but Falmouth (soon to be Portland) Harbor remained a bustling port thanks to the activities of privateers. Merchants from Falmouth and elsewhere built ships here in anticipation of the new business of capturing enemy cargo. John Fox and Benjamin Titcomb invested in a ship they called the *Fox*. Fitted with only four iron guns, the ship wasn't well prepared for capturing a British merchant vessel, but they sent it out anyway. Only eight days later, the *Fox* came upon an enemy merchant ship fitted with eighteen guns. Luckily, the *Fox* had the element of surprise and captured the ship with its valuable cargo, including indigo and deerskins. It was a happy day when the *Fox* sailed its prize into Boston Harbor—and a very lucrative one for Fox and Titcomb.

THE *RAPID* IS SEIZED AND SEIZED AGAIN

In 1808, Portland merchant William Jewett built a brig that he named the *Rapid* and embarked on dangerous missions, trying to run French blockades of English colonies in the West Indies and English blockades of French ones. The risks were high, but so were the rewards. Jewett himself was along for the voyage when he purchased a cargo of cotton in South Carolina to sell in Europe. He didn't find the price he was hoping for in Falmouth, England, so under the protection of the British navy he sailed for Prussia. By the time the *Rapid* arrived, the city had been captured by Napoleon, and the French seized the vessel. After several days under guard in the harbor at Memel, Jewett and the crew were feeling desperate. They managed to remove the flint from the French soldiers' guns, raise the sails and cut the cables with an axe. With no ammunition, the French found themselves helpless to prevent the captain and crew from taking sail.

When it became apparent that the *Rapid* was going to make its escape, the French went over the side into their own boat, knowing that if they didn't escape, they would become the captives. The *Rapid* managed to sail out of the harbor and make its way to safety at Riga in Latvia, where Jewett finally sold the cargo of cotton and got himself a good price for it. They were forced to spend the winter in the Baltic harbor, but when spring finally came, they sailed back home by way of London. The *Rapid* further enhanced its reputation by making record time from London to Boston—only fifteen days.

Unfortunately for Jewett, the *Rapid* was seized by the British during the War of 1812. The seizure came on the heels of a ten-hour chase by two British frigates that finally ended in the *Rapid*'s capture. The crew members were held prisoner in England for the duration of the war. But the captain of the British ship that had finally captured the *Rapid* was so impressed by Captain Joseph Weeks's sailing skills that he returned Weeks's sword as sign of respect.

THE *DART* FINDS RUM

Within a few weeks after war was declared in 1812, the *Dart* was built, armed and ready for privateering. Only a few days out to sea, Captain Curtis and the crew captured the *Diana* out of London with a cargo of rum bound for Quebec. The cargo was brought back to harbor, where it was quickly pronounced to be some of the finest rum ever made. Due to its distinctive quality, the liquor sold quickly and at a high price in Portland, where the bottles were brought out for special occasions in the finest public houses and private homes. Long after the original bottles had been drunk, "Old Dart Rum" remained legendary. Advertisements for new batches of rum would promise that the liquor came out of the original "Old Dart" casks.

Rum from the *Dart* had a rival in Admiral rum, another particularly fine batch with an unusual history. It was discovered by Captain Lemuel Weeks and his crew in a barnacle-covered puncheon, or cask, floating at sea. Captain Weeks kept the cask for himself and for years treated his closest friends to his special stock.

The *Dash* Sets a Fine Table

The *Dash* had its share of privateering success, making fifteen captures in seven cruises. It once brought in a load of fine coffee, but a warehouse fire on Union Wharf destroyed the cargo. Later, the *Dash* captured the *Teazer*, which was full of high-quality crockery. The ladies of town found the tableware to be a wonderful alternative to the coarse, brown earthenware they usually had to use. Suddenly the tables of many Portland dining rooms were set with fine, cream-colored British dishware.

The capture of the *Peter Waldo*, an English ship out of New Castle, also yielded a cargo of fine crockery. The ship's goods were sold at auction to local shopkeepers, who watched it fly off their shelves. For generations, old Portland families kept the crockery in their collections, sharing the inside joke that it was called "Peter Waldo Ware."

The Collectorship of Customs

When Isaac Ilsley replaced Nathaniel Fosdick as collector of customs, it was the hardest blow in a series of hard blows that he received in 1803. In May of the same year, Fosdick had suffered one of the worst robberies in Portland's history. "On Monday or Tuesday evening some daring villain entered the house of Nathaniel Fosdick, Esquire and took there from a portable desk containing about ten thousand dollars and a number of valuable papers," reported the *Portland Gazette* at the end of May. Two or three hundred dollars of the money was in gold coin, with the rest in paper from various banks. The empty desk was

Enoch Ilsley's residence at India and Middle Street (house built in 1784; photo circa 1890). *Courtesy of the Portland Public Library Special Collections and Archives.*

found later in the stable. Fosdick offered $1,000 for any information regarding the theft and promised to give the reward to the thief himself upon return of the money, "no questions shall be asked, nor the name of the person ever disclosed," he promised. He was willing to pay $500 to see the thief brought to justice even if he couldn't retrieve the money.

The theft, as awful as it was, was not Fosdick's only problem that year. His very lucrative political appointment was about to be pulled out from under him. Ever since the "People's President," Thomas Jefferson, had taken office, Fosdick's career had been in jeopardy. It wasn't easy being a Federalist serving in Jefferson's Democratic-Republican administration; it wasn't easy being an Episcopalian in Puritan-dominated Portland, and it wasn't easy remaining popular after you charge some of the leading citizens with customs violations.

Fosdick was quite sure that the wealthy and influential Deering family held a grudge against him for his part in apprehending John Deering for attempted smuggling. It didn't help Fosdick's cause that Edward Preble, one of the nation's most influential naval commanders, was now married to Mary Deering. Fosdick knew that Preble had the ear of Secretary of War

Henry Dearborn. To an outsider like Fosdick, the connections between the upper-class Portland merchant families wove a dangerous web. Isaac Ilsley, of the successful rum merchant and distillery family, had furthered his interests when his cousin Almira married James Deering. It certainly was in the interests of the Ilsley family to put one of their own in the position of customs collector, Fosdick's supporters observed wryly.

But when Ilsley was assigned to replace him, Fosdick did not go down without a fight. Convinced that he could put up a good argument to regain his job, Fosdick traveled to Washington, D.C., to plead his case.

Meanwhile, Edward Preble lent his efforts to the campaign in support of Ilsley. Though he tried to remain behind the scenes, Preble wrote a letter to the secretary of war in support of Ilsley and against Fosdick. "I understand that Mr. Fosdick is in Washington to endeavor to regain his office," he wrote to Dearborn, "and that he took with him a letter or remonstrance signed by a number of the inhabitants of Portland." Preble dismissed Fosdick's backers as his "bottle companions," and he claimed that Fosdick was "an enemy to the President and whole of his administration."

Nathaniel Fosdick did not succeed in getting his job back. He probably moved away from Portland at this point. No record seems to exist to indicate that he ever apprehended the thief or regained his $10,000.

Once he obtained the position, Isaac Ilsley remained firmly entrenched as customs collector for many years. During the War of 1812, he was instrumental in seizing the U.S. brig *Holon* for carrying $22,000 in British goods into Portland Harbor. He built a fine brick house on Spring Street, and the family rum business thrived. He did not retire as U.S. customs collector until 1829.

The Rum Years

"They have a custom of…now and then drinking a dram of the bottle extraordinarily," John Jocelyn reported regarding the early inhabitants of Casco Bay in 1670. In the seventeenth century, New Englanders discovered that molasses could be fermented into alcohol, and rum became the liquor of choice. Ships with cargos of shooks, the barrel staves needed by the sugar cane processors, would sail out of Portland Harbor to the Caribbean and return with West Indian rum or molasses. By the end of the eighteenth century, Portland had its own distilleries, and in 1803, Daniel Ilsley obtained a patent for his operation on Distillery Wharf, where business thrived. Ilsley

City hall, built in 1825. From *Centennial Celebration*.

promised that his new methods would "produce spirits of a better quality and in greater quantity and in less time." The Ilsley family members were ready to compete against the rum-makers of the Caribbean, creating high-proof liquor "equal in flavor to any which is imported and entirely free from that disagreeable smell and taste which has rendered the rum of this country inferior to that of the West Indies." The Ilsleys were proud of their home brew, and so was the rest of Portland.

In the early part of the 1800s, rum was pervasive in the city's social life. Every grocery store provided a cask from which customers could serve

Neal Dow (1804–1897). From *Portland, Past and Present* (compiled 1899).

themselves. During gatherings, such as militia musters, venders would sell gingerbread, molasses candy and rum punch, not just to the men but to the women and children in the crowd as well. Rum was served at agricultural fairs, fireman's parades, cattle shows and even town meetings. Rum was even sold inside the courthouse. At eleven o'clock in the morning, a bell would ring in Portland, and laborers would take a break with salt fish, crackers and rum. At home, the good host always offered the liquor to his guests, and even the local ministers would have been considered rude not to accept the offering. Rum was served at wakes, sometimes with a decanter and glasses displayed on the coffin for the mourners to help themselves. At sea, navy and merchant sailors counted on their daily rum ration.

Thanks to the long tradition of trade with the West Indies, Portlanders had better and cheaper access to rum than just about anyone else in the country. Their dependence on it eventually led to a backlash that was equally extreme. The temperance movement began to catch on in the 1830s in Portland, gaining momentum and culminating in the Maine Law in 1851 that prohibited the sale of alcohol statewide. Portland swung dramatically from being a center for the distillation, trade and consumption of rum to a city that outlawed it altogether.

Neighborhood Battles

Often I think of the beautiful town
That is seated by the sea;
Often in thought go up and down
The pleasant streets of that dear old town,
And my youth comes back to me.
—*Henry Wadsworth Longfellow, "My Lost Youth"*

Charles Ilsley was ready for a fight. The twelve-year-old and his clan of Lower Enders had drenched their snow fort in water, and it was now an ice fortress. Magazines of ice balls and other missiles were stacked inside, and boys took turns, day and evening, watching for the enemy. Eventually, the Upper Enders arrived, and the Exchange Street battle was on. It was a tough one, and heads got broken. Ilsley loved a fight.

To Ilsley, the entire territory from Munjoy Hill to Bramhall Hill was one big battlefield in 1819. The war with England was over but not forgotten by the young boys who had seen the smoke of warfare when the American *Enterprise* triumphed over England's *Boxer* and watched the funeral procession for the two commanders killed at sea.

Plum Street ran north and south and divided the Neck in two. The Upper Enders were to the east of Plum Street and the Lower Enders to the west. Inside these major alliances were smaller clans: on the Lower End, the High Street boys were high class and snobby—their private school was on Union Street, and Ilsley's Union Street clan had an alliance with them. The High Street boys needed help getting through Gorham Corner because the boys who lived there

Above: Exchange Street. From *Artwork of Portland, Maine* (1894).

Right: Longfellow Memorial, Congress Street, Portland, Maine, erected in 1888. *Photograph by Kate Johnson.*

Portland Savings. From *Portland and Vicinity.*

were a wild set of vagabonds. In return, the High Street boys let the Union Street clan sled on Cross Hill in their neighborhood and helped defend them through Gorham Corner to get there. Ilsley's clan didn't fight with the High Street boys unless there was no one else to fight with. The Dockhams, the ones from down along the wharves on the Lower End, were big and strong, On the other side of the divide, the Clay Covers were tough, just like the Dockhams; the Federal Streeters were bullies and the Hill tribe a dangerous crew. Above High Street were outliers who fought on one side and then another.

Getting home from school in the afternoon was never easy. Ilsley and his friends had to fight their way through. Sometimes a boy would get a

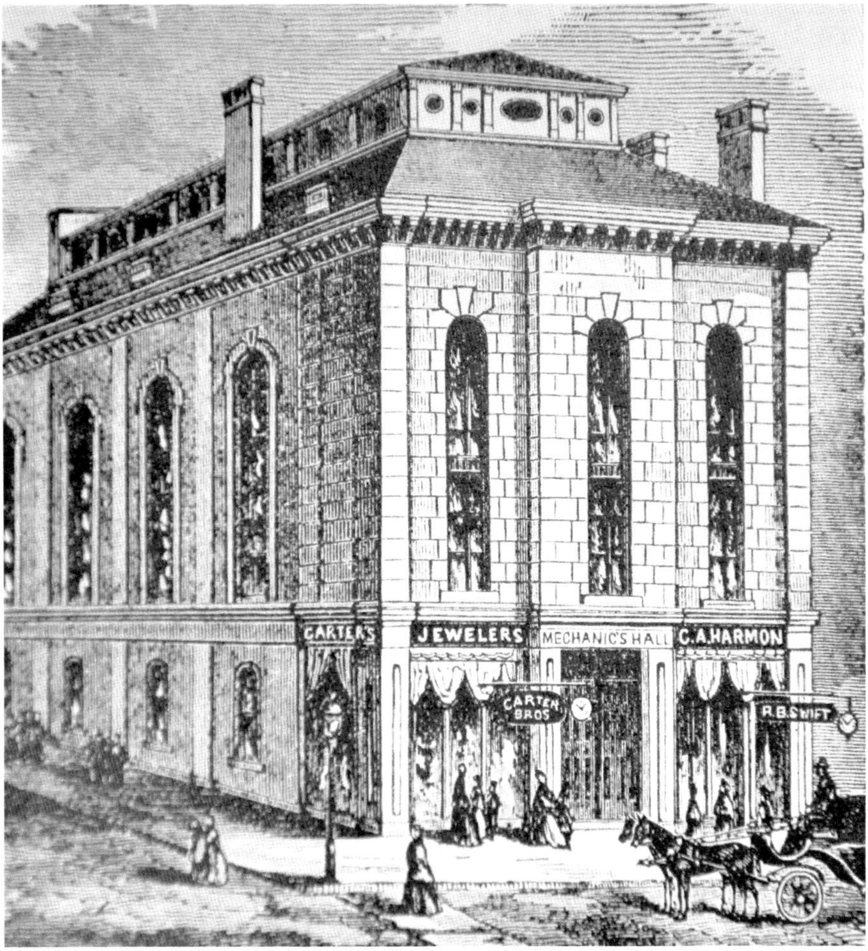

Mechanics Hall. *From Portland and Vicinity.*

bloody nose or a bruise to show for himself, and if he didn't stay alert, he would be sure to get his sled or bat or hoop stolen from him—that is, unless it had thirteen notches carved on it. That was the mark on which they had all agreed. You couldn't take something if had thirteen notches on it. That was the law.

The snowball fight in the field near Exchange Street was the last pitched battle that Ilsley remembered between the Upper Enders and the Lower Enders. It ended in a draw when Portland policemen broke it up. "The fact was, matters had been carried to such a pass that the town authorities thought it high time to interfere, which they did," recalled Ilsley years later.

Ilsley grew out of his rough and pugnacious years and eventually became a poet, novelist and journalist. His boyhood reminiscences appeared in the *Portland Sunday Times* when he was sixty-eight-years-old. They provided a bit of nostalgia for longtime residents, but they also came with a message. The boyhood squabbles had a parallel in the international conflicts of the time, he said. Men are capable of waging war over international issues that are just as frivolous. "Looking calmly back upon those boyish fields, the cause, the grounds of our quarreling appear fully as reasonable as do those which in the majority of cases embroil nations," he concluded.

John B. Brown Climbs the Ladder

John Brown's face was flushed and his eyes flashed as he steadily looked at each of Portland's leading businessmen. "You can go to hell, gentlemen," he said abruptly as he turned and marched out of the conference room.

The directors of the Canal Bank were rattled by Brown's curt response, and it became the talk of Portland. "He turned upon us," director Swan related later in the barbershop, "and, with great vehemence said 'You can go to…" Swan paused. "I won't repeat it," he continued, "but we could go to a country where the temperature is much higher than in Portland."

Soon other bankers in town got wind of the scene that Brown had made, and the story made them uneasy, too. Getting capitalist John Bundy Brown upset would do no one any good. That afternoon, the directors of the city's three largest banks met and worked out a deal. They decided to give Brown the loan that he was asking for by dividing the $50,000 between them so that no bank would have to take all the risk. They sent for Brown to tell him of their decision.

Brown didn't seem surprised. He was used to getting what he wanted. It wasn't because he had been born into wealth. He had not. He had been nothing more than a shop boy in Gray before coming to Portland as a young man. His energy, drive and determination could outlast anyone's, and Portlanders had learned that it was better to be carried along in his wake than to try to stand in his way.

When Brown first arrived in Portland in 1825, he found a job as a clerk at Alpheus Shaw's grocery store. He was quick to learn the trade, and within a few years he had his own business in partnership with St. John Smith. At first, the establishment on Congress Street in the city hall building was nothing more than a typical grocery store. They bartered food for barrel parts, like

John B. Brown's residence. From *Portland and Vicinity.*

hoop poles and shooks, made smart trades and gradually increased their business. By 1845, Smith and Brown had one of the largest retail businesses in the state. Customers all over New Hampshire, Vermont and Maine bought their products and received delivery from Portland by ox and horse carts. The grocery business had expanded to include farm implements, and Brown seemed to have an eye for innovation. He was good at figuring out which newly patented inventions would work best on the farm, and he was capable of convincing retailers and farmers that switching from the old ways to something new was worth a try.

The $50,000 Brown borrowed in the late 1840s came at a pivotal time. He had lost money in his brother-in-law's experimental scheme to make sugar

John B. Brown. From *Portland and Vicinity*.

from molasses. A lot of Portlanders were not surprised when the efforts failed. Molasses was a byproduct of the sugar cane, they said. It's what you have left *after* you process the sugar. How can you make sugar out of *that*? When the business went bankrupt, everyone figured that this would be the end of that idea. But Brown persisted and the timing felt right.

As the temperance movement gained momentum in Portland, the sale of rum declined, and the harbor's long tradition of importing molasses for local distilleries was in jeopardy. Many in Portland feared the decline of the West Indies trade, but few thought that anything could be done about it. Brown was insistent. He knew that there was another use for the molasses. It wasn't long before his employee, Dependence Furbish, came up with the innovation to use steam to turn molasses into sugar.

Brown's Sugar House was born, and it proved to be Brown's most profitable endeavor. By 1850, the company was the largest importer of molasses in New England. The sugar made in Portland was loaded onto Grand Trunk railroad cars and shipped all over the United States and Canada, or it was loaded from one of his three wharves onto steamers bound for Liverpool. Brown invested his profits in railroads and shipping, and his empire grew.

Meanwhile, Brown had his eye on a section of Bramhall Hill on the west end of Portland. It was swampy and covered with low juniper bushes, and no one wanted it. Portlanders were surprised when Brown bought ten acres and commenced a huge building project. In 1856, he erected a mansion and filled it with Italian landscapes by Portland painter John Rollin Tilton, as well as neoclassical sculptures by local artist Franklin Simmons. He put in gardens of rare plants, landscaped shrubbery and hedges. Eventually, his ten acres became a lush compound with his children's houses joining his own.

He nearly always had a gruff and serious expression on his face, and in the winter he wore a coat with a huge fur collar that left no question as to his wealth. He had "an over-bearing, get-out-of-my-way sort of disposition," recalled Portland local John Todd. "When I first knew him, I used to feel I should give him most of the sidewalk when I met him."

Todd also managed to see another side to Brown. A mutual acquaintance was sick and in need of money and asked Todd to intercede for him with Brown. Would he ask Brown for ten dollars?

"I don't like to ask him; I shall not get it," complained Todd.

The friend persuaded him, and so Todd found himself in the formidable man's office. "Good morning, John," Brown said and kept writing. Eventually, he looked up. "What is wanted?"

The Falmouth Hotel. From *Portland and Vicinity.*

When Todd explained, Brown's mood softened. "What? Is he in straightened circumstances?" Brown promptly gave Todd a ten-dollar bill. "Don't let him want for anything. Tell him I will call to see him."

Portlanders were never so grateful to Brown as when he built the Falmouth Hotel. After the terrible destruction of most of Portland's business district in the Fire of 1866, businessmen were discouraged from attempting anything new. Everyone said what Portland needed most to bring it back to life after the devastating fire was a first-class hotel, yet no one was willing to make the investment.

The year following the fire, Brown threw his resources behind the Falmouth Hotel and gave Portlanders something to feel proud of. It was an elegant establishment, and townspeople could boast of the latest innovations: an elevator and bathing rooms on all floors. Visitors and locals alike embraced the place that was known as "the hotel of a million banquets."

Eventually, the times did catch up with Brown's Sugar House. It became outdated when sugar cane countries began refining their molasses themselves. At the same time, sugar cane exporters began to ship their product in bags rather than wooden boxes and no longer had use for Portland's wood products. The strong ties between the West Indies and Portland Harbor weakened, but by then Brown's investments in real estate, transportation and banking were so wide-ranging that he was prepared for the changing times.

"Mr. Brown was born to command, a natural leader of men," recalled Todd, and that remained true until Brown's death in 1881. "I used to hear it said in my shop, 'Is John Brown in favor of it? If so, it will go.'"

John Todd (1821–1911). From *A Sketch of the Life of John M. Todd* (1906).

The Glorious Cause

There are things of which I may not speak;
There are dreams that cannot die;
There are thoughts that make the strong heart weak,
And bring a pallor into the cheek,
And a mist before the eye.
–Henry Wadsworth Longfellow, "My Lost Youth"

The crowd waiting outside the First Parish Church grew bigger and angrier as late afternoon turned into evening. Lydia could hear them grumbling that no New Hampshire Radical or Boston Reformer was going to stand behind this pulpit and preach in this church about putting an end to slavery. When abolitionists Stephen Symonds Foster and John Murray Spear arrived, the mob viciously turned on them. They lunged at Foster, ripped his clothes and punched and clubbed him in the head. Undaunted, Foster and Spear fought their way through the crowd and into the church. With the mob still threatening them at the door, Foster escaped through a window in the back. Helped by some of the other women in Portland's Anti-Slavery Society, Lydia Neal Dennett created a human shield around Foster and escorted him from the back of the church to safety. Once Foster had gotten away, Spear thought that the crowd had calmed down and attempted to leave through the front door. The mob's fury had not lessened. The people attacked Spear and nearly beat him to death. He was taken to the Dennett home, where he took six weeks to recuperate.

The assault on Foster and Spear in 1842 wasn't Portland's first mob scene over the slavery issue. In 1833, British abolitionist George Thompson's appearance at the Quaker meetinghouse had caused a riot. To escape, he dressed in women's clothing and was escorted out by some of the church women. In 1836, a meeting by the Maine Anti-Slavery Society attracted proslavery proponents who threw rocks and attempted to club participants. Many Portlanders disdained the violence but chose to remain quiet. Some remained neutral for political reasons and put their commitment to states' rights above the slavery issue. Moderates often favored the colonization movement and sought to send freed slaves back to Africa. Most churches of the time either ignored the issue or used biblical passages to defend slavery. Portland was a city of ship owners, merchants and dockworkers, all of whom had ties to the South and to the cotton trade. Some had even quietly fitted out their vessels as slave ships.

In the 1830s, when Lydia and her husband, Oliver, first began to organize for the abolition of slavery, they were considered fanatics by most people

First Parish Church, built in 1825. *Photo by Luann Yetter.*

in Portland. Quakers like Lydia Dennett were used to facing controversy. In 1740, the Puritans in the Portland area had observed a day of fasting and prayer to demonstrate their opposition to Quakerism. Yet despite their unpopularity with a number of conventional denominations, the group slowly grew. By the time Lydia was born in 1798, the congregation had a brick building on the corner of Federal and Pearl Streets that served as its meetinghouse. Quakers were peace-loving people but could sometimes be forceful in spreading their views. Four Quakers once attended a service at the First Parish defiantly wearing their hats inside the church and speaking their minds. They "sat with their hats on all the forenoon and then harangued," complained Pastor Deane. Quakers' antiwar stance was often seen as unpatriotic. They refused to fight in the War for Independence and the War of 1812. By the 1830s, many of the Quakers had found a new cause: the antislavery movement.

Quakers and others who favored immediate emancipation for slaves were considered radicals. Still, Lydia was not afraid to speak her mind. She was known as a fine storyteller and an eloquent speaker. It had been her stately appearance alongside Foster that had helped shield him from the mob. In their home on Spring Street, the Dennetts corresponded with and entertained the leaders of the abolition movement, including William Lloyd Garrison and Frederick Douglass.

The Dennett house was also a station on the Underground Railroad. At great risk to themselves and their standing in the community, the Dennetts opened their home to escaped slaves who were desperately trying to make

William Pitt Fessenden. From *Portland and Vicinity.*

their way to safety in Canada or England. In 1848, the Dennetts took in Ellen and William Craft, escaped slaves from Macon, Georgia. Ellen was very light-skinned and could pass for white. She traveled from the South dressed in men's clothing, pretending to be a white man traveling north to treat his rheumatism. Her husband, William, played the role of her slave. She did not know how to write, so she kept her right arm in a sling and used this as an excuse not to sign hotel registers. When the couple arrived in Portland, they found that the steamer they had intended to take had been delayed. Their dangerous journey was slowed down by a few days, and they stayed hidden at the Dennetts' home. William Craft later called Oliver Dennett "one of the best and most hospitable men in the state." The Crafts were grateful to Lydia and Oliver for the risks they took on their behalf. "By simply fulfilling the scripture injunction, to take in the stranger…he ran the risk of incurring a penalty of $2000 and twelve months' imprisonment," wrote William later. "But neither the Fugitive Slave Law, nor any other satanic enactment, can ever drive the spirit of liberty and humanity out of such noble and generous-hearted men."

George Ropes, shopkeeper and cutlery manufacturer, also provided a station on the Underground Railroad. Early one Sunday morning, an escaped slave appeared at his door, trembling and agitated. He had seen his master in Boston and had fled in a panic. He did not even want to rest long enough to eat. He jumped in fright at the opening of a door. The antislavery society kept a fine pair of horses and a closed carriage for such situations. The fugitive was soon transported out of Portland and was on his way to Canada.

Samuel Fessenden was another member of the antislavery movement. To many Portlanders, his opinions about blacks seemed extreme. Most Portland professionals shied away from such controversial topics, but Fessenden proclaimed boldly and frequently that he supported "the glorious cause…that of promoting the emancipation of three million of our fellow beings from a degradation and oppression more cruel than was ever endured by an equal number in any age of the world." Fessenden made friends among the twenty-odd families who had established the Abyssinian Congregational Church on Munjoy Hill. He invited these black church members into his home, visited them in theirs and supported their education and business projects.

Antislavery people needed to keep quiet about such things, but word spread that Fessenden was active in the Underground Railroad and that fugitive slaves came to him for cash and aid on their way to Canada. Fessenden had

Dow Street. From *Portland and Vicinity.*

a thriving law practice in Portland. His confident style, forthright, honest expression and dark-haired good looks made him likeable, and his skill with a jury made him a popular lawyer despite his unorthodox views when it came to race issues. When the fugitive slave law was passed in 1850, he refused to keep a low profile about it. At the barbershop, he was quick to state his opinion. "I want you to advertise it throughout the city," he told his barber, "that Samuel Fessenden spits upon that law and tramples it under his feet, and never will obey it!"

"Do you advise people to violate the laws that Congress passes?" his barber, John Todd, asked incredulously.

"I do advise it," he answered. "When a man, rich or poor, bond or free, calls at my door and asks for bread, he will get it sure, in spite of the fugitive slave law that forbids it."

The Prince of Wales

No one in the crowds lining India Street remembered the October day in 1775 when the British bombardment destroyed Portland. Some remembered the War of 1812, the battle between the *Enterprise* and the *Boxer* that was fought off the coast of Maine and the funeral procession for the warring American and British commanders that took place on the same streets. Since those tumultuous times, Portlanders' minds had become less focused on England and more intent on their own country, the widening gulf between the North and the South, the contentious issue of slavery and the westward expansion that was beginning to lure some of Portland's young people to the inland wilderness.

On this crisp October day, everyone's minds had turned again to England as they eagerly awaited the arrival of the Prince of Wales. Edward VII, son of Queen Victoria, was eighteen years old and was completing a four-month American tour with a final stop in Portland, Maine. Portlanders had been reading reports of the tour with interest. Prince Edward was an affable young man, the newspapers said, and he had charmed the American people wherever he went. The crowds lining the streets of Portland for his procession were proud that he had chosen their town as the last stop on his tour.

The prince's visit attracted attention from the outlying areas, and trains full of excited royal-watchers arrived at the station on the waterfront's new Commercial Street. Horses and buggies poured in on every road. Flags flew on city buildings from the customhouse to Mechanic's Hall and decorated the bridle of nearly every horse on every street.

State Street, from Congress Street. From *Portland and Vicinity*.

"Munjoy." *Drawing by Sara Tarbox.*

The prince arrived from Boston by train in the early afternoon. The crowd cheered as he stepped from his car and yelled even more wildly when he lifted his hat and bowed. He was dressed simply in a blue frock coat, cravat, light gray pants and top hat. "He's dressed rather plainly," some whispered.

"His hat is a bit dated," noted others. There was nothing particularly regal about the Prince of Wales, and the crowd was soon taken by the young man's easygoing manner. The prince's clothing was ordinary, but the railroad car he had arrived in was not. It had been decorated on orders from the directors of the Eastern Railroad in a way they thought would be fit for a prince. The walls were adorned with gold, crimson and cinnamon woven silk, oversized mirrors and coats of arms from Massachusetts, New Hampshire and Maine. Blue silk studded with stars covered the ceiling. The prince and his entourage could lounge on Turkish sofas and eat with a magnificent set of silverware. "Everything about the car was furnished in a style of royal excellence," gushed *Eastern Argus* editor John Adams. "It was the most magnificent one we have ever seen."

The prince, Lord Lyons and the Duke of Newcastle were welcomed by Portland mayor Joseph Howard, who soon became the luckiest man in Maine that day. The prince's carriage was followed by five more that carried the rest of his entourage. "God Save the Queen" played as the carriages proceeded up India Street, and the prince was saluted by companies from the area regiments. The procession moved through cheering crowds, and the Portland Rifle Corps acted as royal guard. The prince responded with an occasional bow. The cheering continued as his carriages traveled along the Eastern Promenade to Victoria Wharf. The prince and his company

Asa Clapp (1805–1891). From *History of Cumberland Co., Maine.*

The Odd Fellows Hall, 1881. *Courtesy of the Portland Public Library Special Collections and Archives.*

disembarked from their carriages and walked through an arch of evergreen onto the wharf. Someone from the crowd threw him a bouquet of flowers that he gamely tried to catch, losing his hat in the process. As he boarded the boat that would take him to his ship, dozens of sails suddenly unfurled on the vessels around him as if by magic. Many exclaimed that the effect of the salute was unlike anything they had witnessed before.

The ceremony was not yet over. The prince was rowed to his ship, the *Hero*, and the royal standard was hoisted to a huge cheer. As Edward VII stepped onto the deck of his royal ship, a twenty-one-gun royal salute boomed through the harbor. Many of the thousands of onlookers remained to watch the *Hero* as it sailed out of harbor, between the breakwater and Hog Island ledge, toward the open seas and England.

Portland's Slave Trader

From his position on the bench, Judge Shipman looked Gordon in the eye as he passed his sentence. "Think of the sufferings of the unhappy beings whom you crowded on the *Erie*," he lectured, "of their helpless agony and terror as you took them from their native land."

No one was sure if Portlander Nathaniel Gordon ever repented his sins as a slave trader. Until the end, he seemed more intent on ruing his bad luck in becoming the first American to hang for the crime than the crime itself. For forty years, slave trading had been an act of piracy in the United States, punishable by death, but the authorities had looked the other way. Now in 1861, at the beginning of the Civil War, the United States Navy had arrested Gordon, the Southern District of New York jury had declared him guilty and President Abraham Lincoln had refused to commute his sentence.

"It becomes my painful duty," wrote Lincoln, "to admonish the prisoner that, relinquishing all expectation of pardon by human authority, he refer himself alone to the mercy of the common God and Father of all men."

Thirty-five years earlier, Gordon was born in Portland to a respectable family, the fourth Nathaniel in an unbroken line. His father was a merchant sea captain and his mother, Mary, a devoted member of the High Street Congregational Church. He had an older sister, Dorcas, and a younger sister named Mary. A bright boy and a good student, his parents had hoped that he would stay in school and perhaps even pursue a profession. Living in a harbor city like Portland and watching his father go off to sea created a pull that was hard for Gordon to resist. At fifteen, he left his books behind and became a merchant seaman. He worked hard and avoided heavy drinking,

Homestead of the late Asa Clapp (circa 1840). From *History of Cumberland Co., Maine* (1880).

two traits that gave him a good reputation with employers, and at twenty he was promoted to captain of his own ship. He was an up-and-coming young man in the city of Portland, and many commented on his energy and ability. "He'll make a fortune, and that right speedily," they said of the young man.

For several years, Gordon sailed out of his hometown and eventually became part owner of a ship. Despite his success, he became restless. Even though he had property valued at several thousand dollars, he felt that he wasn't amassing a fortune fast enough. He sailed to California hoping to find gold but soon became disillusioned with his prospects there. It was upon his return that he met some businessmen who lured him into the slave trade by promising him that he could make a lot of money. He agreed to work with them and made three slave trading voyages. One trip was only marginally successful, but the other two proved hugely profitable. There was indeed money to be made, even if the penalties could be severe. "The navigators and shipping men have lost their sense of the wickedness of the trade," observed the *New York Times*.

In 1855, at the age of twenty-eight, Gordon married Elizabeth Annie Kenney, who was then only sixteen. Two years later, the couple had a son, Nathaniel, the fifth in line, and they made their home with his mother

Commercial Street mural, street scene, circa 1880. *Photo by Luann Yetter.*

on Danforth Street. Gordon probably didn't seem wicked to his Portland neighbors. If they suspected that he had made money in the slave trade, they probably kept their suspicions to themselves.

On his fourth voyage, in the summer of 1860, Gordon captained the *Erie* out of Havana, Cuba, for the west coast of Africa with a cargo of liquor. He arrived at the Congo River and exchanged the liquor for nearly nine hundred slaves. Gordon promised his crew one dollar per head for every slave landed alive in Cuba. They densely packed their human cargo below deck and set sail back toward Havana. He hoped to sell the slaves to sugar plantations at a good price.

"Think of the cruelty and wickedness of seizing nearly a thousand fellow-beings," Judge Shipman admonished Gordon at his sentencing, "who never did you harm, and thrusting them beneath the decks of a small ship, beneath a burning tropical sun, to die of disease or suffocation, or be transported to distant lands, and be consigned, they and their posterity, to a fate far more cruel than death."

The *Erie* had only sailed about fifty miles from the coast when it was captured by the USS *Mohican* and taken to Monrovia, where all of Gordon's surviving captives were released. Gordon was convicted in November and awaited his hanging in Manhattan's House of Detention—a dank, dirty facility widely known as the Tombs. While imprisoned there, he was visited by his mother. She brought him letters from Reverend Chickering and the reverend's wife, both from Portland's High Street Congregational Church. The letters from Mrs. Chickering "seemed to make him quite thoughtful and serious," according to prison clergyman Amzi Camp. Gordon remained hopeful of a pardon, and many among both friends and foes predicted that since the penalty had never been enforced, "they dare not hang him."

On the last day of January, Lincoln issued General War Order No. 1, which called for all United States naval and land forces to begin a general advance by February 22. A few days later, Lincoln announced that he would not grant Gordon a pardon and set the date of the hanging for February 21.

According to the *New York Times*, on Mary Gordon's last visit to her son, she "commanded his soul to an all-wise and all-loving Savior…and then with one long tender embrace she burst into an agony of grief and left the

Looking down High Street. From *Portland and Vicinity*.

room." His wife Elizabeth's last visit was the day before the hanging and even more emotional. Even after Lincoln's letter, she had clung to the notion that her husband would somehow be pardoned, and the reality of their situation did not seem to hit her until that final visit. "She fell fainting at his feet," reported the *New York Times,* and "reviving, she gave way to the most agonizing cries, and clung to him with an intensity which seemed to say never, never will I let you go."

In the midst of her grief, she also might have slipped him a vial of poison, for it was discovered later that he had somehow taken strychnine. Gordon's final hours were agonizing for him. The poison gave him convulsions, lockjaw and other "torments of the most terrible nature" that doctors treated by pumping his stomach and administering large quantities of whiskey. Though he acted drunk at the hanging, Gordon managed to speak for himself. "I die with the clear conscience of a man who has done, intentionally, no wrong," he said. He accused the prosecutor of lying to the jury, a claim that the court transcript could easily refute. Before the marshal drew the black cap over his eyes, Gordon said, "Well, a man can't die but once: I'm not afraid."

"And thus the majesty of the law has been vindicated," the *New York Times* editorialized, "and the stamp of the gallows has been set upon the crime of slave-trading in so forcible a way that it will not soon be forgotten."

A Daring Enterprise

Lieutenant Dudley Davenport was lying in his berth in the U.S. government cutter *Caleb Cushing* at about midnight when he heard something overhead. All seemed quiet as he climbed to the deck when suddenly arms reached out of the darkness to grab him. "You are now a prisoner of the Confederate navy," a voice said in a Southern accent. As his eyes adjusted to the darkness, Davenport could see the outlines of four or five pistols, all pointed at his head. There was nothing he could do to resist as the Confederates fastened irons around his wrists.

"No harm will come to the crew if you surrender peaceably," one of the soldiers told him. "But if you don't, we've got orders to blow every man's brains out who shows any fight." With those words in mind, Davenport's crew submitted to arrest and to the irons. They were ordered to the berth deck, and from there they could feel their ship moving and knew that they were sailing down harbor. Some of the Confederates stayed below deck, and Davenport watched them rummage through his things until they came upon his watch and chain.

"That's mine!" he exclaimed.

The Confederate soldier handed him the watch. "Your private property should be respected," he said and gave him a cigar as well.

The next morning, the soldiers took Davenport to the captain's cabin. Sitting in Davenport's chair was the Confederate in command, who introduced himself as Lieutenant C.W. Reed. Davenport was surprised to see how young he looked; even with his mustache and whiskers, the captain didn't look over twenty-five. He was slim, with a narrow face and a gentlemanly demeanor.

Portland Observatory in the 1840s. From *With Pen and Ink.*

"I'm sorry lieutenant, to meet you under these circumstances, but this is one of the fortunes of war." Davenport nodded. "You being a Southern man ought to ashamed of yourself!" Reed continued.

Davenport winced. He didn't know how Reed knew this, but he wished that it weren't common knowledge that he had been born in Georgia. Since the beginning of the rebellion, his Southern roots had led to all kinds of suspicion. But this was no time for argument. "You have acted humanely sir," Davenport answered, "and in case we are taken I'll represent you favorably to the U.S. authorities." He hoped they would be taken. By now, he thought, everyone in Portland must know that their U.S. Revenue Service cutter is missing from Portland Harbor.

The disappearance of the cutter *had* been discovered, and the city was in a panic. Rumors circulated wildly. One rumor had the Southerner Davenport and some of his crew sailing off to join the Confederacy. Another story had the cutter seized by Southern rebels who had snuck into enemy territory disguised as fishermen.

Either way, their country was in a war. Even with no warship in the harbor, the Portlanders were determined to recapture the *Cushing*. Infantrymen from Fort Preble quickly commissioned the cruise ship steamer *Forest City*, frantically

Customhouse, circa 1850. *Courtesy of the Portland Public Library Special Collections and Archives.*

fitting it up with guns and armament. Shortly before noon, it steamed out of harbor in hot pursuit. Close behind the *Forest City* was the passenger steamer *Chesapeake*, manned by volunteers from the city of Portland. John B. Brown, Portland's wealthiest merchant, had quickly chartered the steamer. Two civilians, Customs Collector Jedediah Jewett and Mayor Jacob McLellan, took charge of preparations. With considerable ingenuity, the volunteers quickly turned the steamer into a battleship. Bales of cotton along the sides and engines made the ship shot-proof. Two menacing brass guns were placed at the bow. The eager volunteers were given muskets and ammunition, and as the *Chesapeake* left the wharf about an hour behind the *Forest City*, the men were cheered by hundreds of well-wishers.

From the Portland Observatory, the *Cushing* had been spotted twelve miles from Bang Island. Naval Inspector William Leighton, commanding the *Chesapeake*, put the course for south half-east past Portland Light. Soon both the *Forest City* and the *Chesapeake* were closing in on the stolen cutter—their steam power, and the lack of wind, enabling them to outpace it. Unsure of who was sailing the *Cushing* or why, the commanders decided to take direct action by sailing up to approach and ask its intentions, but before they could do so, the *Cushing* opened fire.

"That means business," said Captain Leighton. "Steer for her, and we'll run her down or go to the bottom."

With the *Cushing* still firing, the *Chesapeake* and the *Forest City* brazenly closed in, intent on striking or boarding the enemy ship. Suddenly one, and then two, boats were lowered from the cutter. Leighton feared that the Rebels planned to board them. Then smoke began to rise from the *Cushing*.

"They have set her on fire!" someone yelled in surprise.

"Sink the devils!" yelled another.

Just then, Leighton spied a white handkerchief elevated from one of the small boats. "The first man that fires shall be shot," he called. "I am not a pirate to fire on a flag of truce!"

When the first small boat rowed up alongside the *Chesapeake*, the crew recognized Davenport looking very agitated. Was he traitor or victim?

Davenport's anger seemed to answer the question. "It is hard, after a man has been taken a prisoner, ironed, and his life threatened by pirates, to be shot by his own friends!" were his first words as he came on board. The irons on the wrists of his crew were good evidence that Davenport told the truth. They had been captured by Rebels, the *Cushing* men quickly explained. And now the Rebels intended to sink their prize.

The *Forest City* took on board the Rebels from the other small boats. They were shackled by the steamer's black steward, and the Confederates complained, not about being captured but about the indignity of being put in chains by a black man. The Yankees were not sympathetic.

The *Cushing* had been abandoned. Davenport explained that the Rebels had not found the four hundred pounds of gunpowder stored on the *Cushing*. Despite threats, he and his crew had refused to reveal where it was. The *Cushing* had been set ablaze, and before long, the fire would find powder. The captains determined that it would be impossible to save the ship without jeopardizing lives. Powerless to act, they could do nothing but watch. After about an hour, the crew members saw what they had been waiting for. "A terrific explosion shakes the heavens," recalled John Adams shortly afterward:

> *The smoke roles up in vast columns, fragments of shells, masts and spars, and blackened timbers are seen hundreds of feet in the air, falling all around. The cutter begins to sink, her stern disappears, the guns roll off the deck into the fathomless deep. She careens, then gives one lurch—and the* Caleb Cushing *sinks beneath the waves. The only remaining mast disappears, but soon rises some fifteen or twenty feet above the water, then sinks to rise no more.*

The *Chesapeake* and the *Forest City* steamed back to Portland, the men eager to tell the tale of rescuing the crew of the *Cushing* and capturing the

Commercial Street mural, wharf scene, circa 1880. *Photo by Luann Yetter.*

Rebel pirates. Reed and his men were imprisoned at Fort Preble, where they revealed the circumstances leading up to their capture of the *Cushing*. They had been privateering along the New England coast for weeks with much success, Reed explained. A graduate of Annapolis, Reed was a skillful commander and had captured twenty-two Union vessels. The less valuable of the ships he destroyed. "Burnt her" he would say with a sly smile as he related the name of a particular ship and its fate. The best ships he kept for himself, trading up each time he captured a better vessel.

Portlanders shook their heads in disbelief as word spread about what Reed's intentions had been. Stealing the *Caleb Cushing* had been only part of his plan. He had hoped for an all-out Confederate assault, burning the two gunboats under construction at Franklin Wharf and then setting fire to the city itself before making a quick escape in the *Cushing*.

Luckily for the city of Portland, the Rebels had been unable to steal into the harbor as early as they had planned. Moonlight had illuminated it, and there was more activity than they had anticipated. They scaled back their plan to merely capturing the *Cushing*. Then a lack of wind had hindered their escape. The wind had been blowing the day before but had ceased just

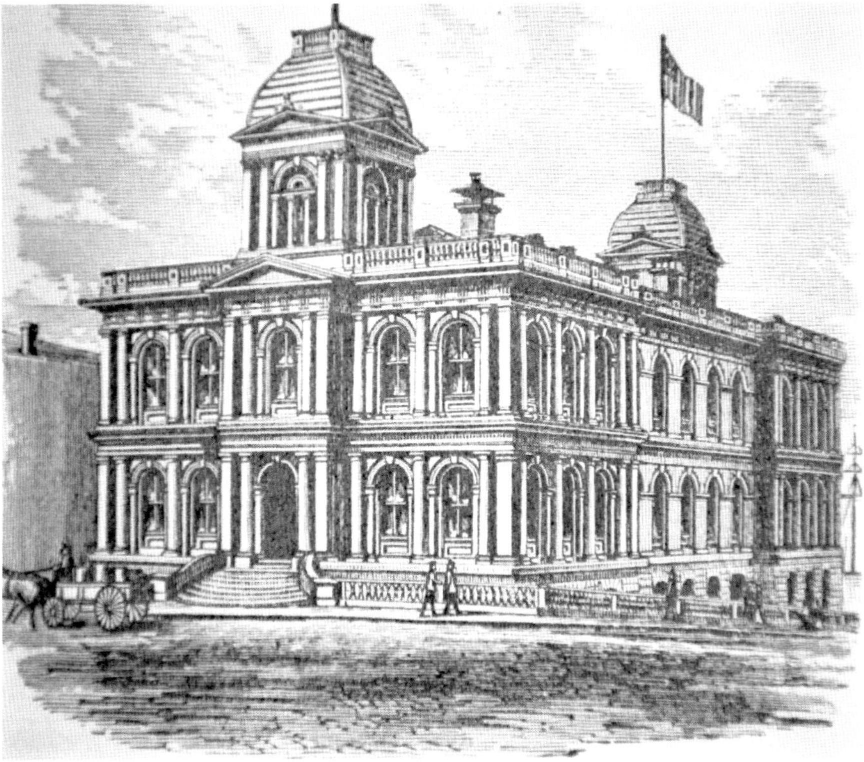

The customhouse. From *Portland and Vicinity.*

when the Rebels needed it to hasten their getaway. Some said that it was the hand of an "Intelligent Power" that stilled the wind that day, as it picked up again right after the Rebels were captured.

A few weeks later, the Confederate prisoners of war were transferred to Fort Warren in Boston Harbor. They were traded for Northern prisoners two years later. Captain Reed, however, was kept in the county jail in Portland. Enemy or not, many Portlanders were charmed by his youthful good nature. "He was a jolly fellow," recalled barber John Todd, "and everyone who met him liked him."

He would not have been so fondly remembered had his plan worked and he had burned the city, as Mowatt had during the Revolutionary War nearly one hundred years before. This time, the wind had been on the Yankees' side. The "Slaveholder's Rebellion" ended three years after the adventure of the *Caleb Cushing.* But a year after that, the winds would blow in Portland. This time the fire would ignite, and the flames would spread.

The Terrible Conflagration

Portlanders celebrated Independence Day in 1866 with a parade in the morning, and they were looking forward to fireworks after dark. The organizers were promising that it would be the most brilliant display ever exhibited in Maine. And it was—brilliant and terrible.

In late afternoon, the fire bells sounded, and soon residents could smell smoke coming from the area around Brown's Wharf. Rumors spread that some boys celebrating with firecrackers had accidentally set fire to one of the boatyards. Strong winds blew from the south, and fear spread with the flames. At first, no one worried about Brown's Sugar House, even though the burning boatyard was right next door. The Sugar House was built with brick and had a slate roof, so everyone assumed that it would be safe from the flames. When it caught fire that evening, fear gave way to shock and panic. The winds were now at gale force, the fire traveling so fast that it was impossible to stop. When it reached Middle Street, the strong winds blew flames like rolling waves from one side to the other. There was no telling what the flames would take out or what they would spare. The fire destroyed every building surrounding Emery and Waterhouse's hardware store but left it standing.

The flames rolled on the wind to Exchange Street, where observers were sure that the customhouse and post office could withstand their heat. But the fire raged through the granite buildings and found its way into the wooden frames. On Congress Street, shopkeepers and residents frantically stashed their valuables and furniture in the city hall, sure that the new stone building would withstand anything. After all, its iron staircases, brick partitions and halls of marble tile were built to last forever. But the brick acted like an oven,

The Fire of 1866, looking up Exchange Street from Fore Street. *Courtesy of the Portland Public Library Special Collections and Archives.*

and the wooden interior eventually reached its flash point. City and county offices, and everyone's valuables, were reduced to ash. "Wooden structures vanished as it were in a moment; piles of brick and stone, *almost* fireproof it was thought, resisted for an instant its onward march, and then were wrapped in a seething, hissing mass of flame," reported Portland's *New York Times* correspondent. The fire raged through the night, up Congress Street and onto Poplar Street, finally burning itself out in the pastures of Munjoy Hill. But by then the wind had reversed itself, so below Cumberland Street firemen battled blazes well into the next day.

Exhausted residents surveyed the damage in the daylight of a new morning. In some ways, they counted their blessings, the major one being that it seemed that there had been no loss of life. Also, the fire had spared the First Parish Church on Congress Street. Somehow the buildings in the Irish Quarter, old and wooden, burned less fiercely than most of the neighborhoods around it. The telegraph office was burned, but the superintendent had quickly moved the equipment to Lancaster Hall, where it survived. Even though wires were down, operators were stationed at the depots, where the telegraph lines ran along the train tracks, and communication continued.

"Nothing can be done in the city today except to take care of the homeless, and that is actively being done. Everybody's latch string hangs out," reported the *New York Times* correspondent. Volunteers from outlying regions flooded into the town on special trains to distribute food. "A cheerful and buoyant feeling prevails," he reported.

Portlanders remained positive in the face of unbelievable destruction. Their city was unrecognizable. "The lines of the street can hardly be traced," the *New York Times* reported. "A space of one and a half miles long, by a quarter of a mile wide, appears like a forest of chimneys, with fragments of walls attached to them…it is impossible to tell where the people lived, the destruction is so complete." The worst of the flames had been extinguished, but remains smoldered everywhere and coal that had been stored in now-destroyed houses continued to burn. Stonework peeled from the exterior of the customhouse, while the interior still smoked and occasionally blazed up again. Firemen,

Middle Street in ruins after the Fire of 1866. From *Portland and Vicinity.*

including volunteers from surrounding towns, continued to work in the ruins. Not a building was standing on Exchange Street. All the banks in the city were gone. All the newspaper offices were gone. About 1,500 buildings in all had been destroyed by the fire, and 1,200 people had lost their homes.

"Thousands of our people are homeless and hungry," Portland's mayor wrote in a message to Boston. "Can you send us some bread and cooked provisions?" Boston sent five carloads of food in response. The federal government sent 1,500 tents to house the homeless.

While most people flooding into Portland were there to help, a few opportunists showed up to take advantage of the situation. "Parties of roughs from the large cities are here and will try to make a raid on our banks," said the reporter. But citizen volunteers and a militia company from Fort Preble were patrolling the streets to guard against anyone trying to steal what was left in the ruins. "The treasure is thoroughly guarded, and if the attempt is made, they will be returned feet foremost," warned the reporter. Lesser crimes like pickpocketing were also problems. With no safe place for their cash, many people were carrying large quantities of money, and according to the reporter, the city was "filled with pick pockets from Boston and New York." Moses Russell had his pocket picked of $1,500; a man on Middle Street was robbed of $400.

Estimates of building and property losses ran into the millions. Wealthy Sugar House owner John B. Brown's losses, which included real estate all over the city, were estimated at $1 million, with insurance covering about half that. Hartford, Connecticut insurance companies sent their adjusters to Portland immediately, and investors all over the country took an interest in their losses. Sale of stock in insurance companies was temporarily halted as the damage was assessed, and at least one insurance company announced immediately that it would not be paying its next semiannual dividend because of the losses.

Within a few days, word of the devastating fire had traveled throughout the United States and Canada and had generated much sympathy. In cities like Boston, New York and St. Louis, committees were formed immediately to raise funds for the fire victims. Trains from Sherbrooke, Montreal and Ottawa arrived with donations of food and blankets.

About ninety years earlier, at the beginning of the Revolutionary War, Portland had been destroyed by fire when the British navy bombarded the town. Once again, the city had been ravaged by flame. Yet townspeople showed an amazing optimism in the face of destruction. "At any rate, we are happy in the belief that such a blow cannot be expected to strike thrice in a century as all the old and dangerous buildings are swept out clear," observed the reporter. "The city will be rebuilt with the greatest attention to future security."

The Irish-African Bishop

Before the Civil War, in his boyhood home in Georgia, James Healy had been considered a Negro slave with no human rights. In 1875, Bishop Healy was one of Portland's leading citizens.

Waves of Irish, Italian and French Canadian immigrants arrived in Protestant New England in the latter part of the 1800s, bringing with them the old religion and a desire for the traditions of the Latin mass, the Virgin Mary and the sacred mysteries they had known in the Old World. The Catholic Church responded to this influx with new cathedrals, missions, convents and schools. Bishop James Healy oversaw the rapid rise of Catholicism in Maine and New Hampshire, supervising the building projects, welcoming the newcomers and making sure that the needy were cared for. The son of an Irish immigrant himself, Healy could identify with their needs as Catholic newcomers to a predominantly Protestant world. However, Healy's background was far richer and more varied than his Irish name and heritage would have indicated. James Healy's father had married a Negro. She was one-eighth African, and she had been a slave.

Healy's father, Michael, had been a self-made man, arriving penniless from Ireland and working his way up to owning his own plantation near Macon, Georgia. Michael had more than fifty slaves; one of them became his common-law wife when she was sixteen and he was in his early thirties. James was the oldest of their ten children. Knowing that their children could never develop their potential in the South, James's father sent them north for their education. When James was only eight, he left home for a Quaker boarding school in New York. He proved himself to be a good student, and he had the ability to turn his misfortunes into opportunities. James went from boarding school to the College of the Holy Cross in Massachusetts, where he distinguished himself as a scholar and graduated as valedictorian in 1849. He wanted to become a Jesuit, but the American branch of the society was based in the slave state of Maryland. A distinguished college graduate, Healy's accomplishments would mean nothing in Maryland. The son of a female slave was a slave, and Healy was considered property in Maryland. He went instead to the Grand Seminary in Montreal. His remarkable intellectual abilities earned him advancement to St. Suplice in Paris to pursue a doctorate. Thanks to the unenlightened policies that forced him to New York, then Massachusetts, farther north to Montreal and then to Paris, Healy ended up receiving a first-rate international education that even most privileged white Americans could not have hoped to obtain.

Cathedral of the Immaculate Conception, Portland, Maine (erected 1856). From *History of Cumberland Co., Maine.*

In 1866, Healy became a priest in Boston, where he served for more than twenty years. He earned the reputation as a great orator and spoke often on behalf of Irish and Italian Catholic immigrants. His reputation grew as he ministered to cholera and typhoid victims during epidemics. He was promoted to bishop and sent to Portland when he was forty-five years old.

Portlanders knew of Healy's racial heritage, although he seemed intent on keeping quiet about it. Despite his dark skin, he seemed to identify with the Irish part of his heritage rather than the African. Healy tirelessly traveled around his diocese, visiting as many communities as he could. He soon became known as the "children's bishop" for his work with orphans and Civil War widows. In the winter, he would let Portland boys hitch their sleds to his sleigh, and in the summer he would keep cookies and candy in his pockets to hand out to children. His fluency in French endeared himself to the French Canadians in the diocese, and he required his priests to speak both French and English in mixed congregations. While prejudice caused some Portlanders to be initially skeptical, Healy quickly won the respect of townspeople, both Catholic and Protestant.

In 1886, in honor of Portland's centennial, Healy gave a speech outlining the history of Catholicism in Portland. At this point, he was fifty-six years old and had served as bishop for eleven years. Well established as a spokesperson for his religion, he described the struggles and triumphs of his church with pride. He described the first Catholic pastor in Portland, Charles Ffrench, from Galway, Ireland.

"Downtown." *Drawing by Sara Tarbox.*

Ffrench had arrived in Portland in the 1820s with the reputation of a rebel. His father had been a Protestant warden and had disowned his young son for having attended a Catholic mass on Christmas Eve. Ffrench faced other challenges in Portland. "In commencing his labors here," said Healy, "there was little to encourage a priest." The small Catholic congregation was not widely accepted amongst the predominantly Protestant population. "In those days," said Healy, "it was difficult, almost dangerous, to show a kind face or fair dealing to Catholics." They could find no one who would agree to sell them land for a church. Eventually, John Fox risked the ire of his fellow Protestants and sold the Catholics a piece of land on Gray and State Streets. Fox's open-mindedness even extended to making a large donation to their building fund. In 1833, St. Dominic's opened its doors to about 150 members. To celebrate the church's dedication, many Catholic dignitaries traveled to Portland and were lodged at the home of Judge William Preble. Though not a Catholic himself, Preble generously entertained the priests and bishops. These acts of kindness were notable, said Healy, because they were offered at a time when "the name of Catholic was like a badge of ignominy in this town."

Father Ffrench continued to serve in Portland until 1839. "Even now," said Healy in 1886, "the aged residents of Portland delight to tell of the genial and gentle manners which made Father Ffrench a universal favorite, in spite of the prejudices of those days."

Healy went on to describe triumphs and setbacks familiar to all who had lived in Portland in the mid-1800s. The Catholic Church acquired new land on Congress Street and built a chapel, a school and a convent. In May 1866, they laid the cornerstone for new and magnificent cathedral. In July came the Great Fire and with it the destruction of all the buildings on the property. "It was a day of sorrow for thousands in Portland," said Healy. But like most residents who suffered massive losses, the Catholics forged ahead anyway just as soon as the smoke cleared. Father Bacon, then bishop of Portland, "at once set to work to rebuild the cathedral chapel, and such was his energy that at Christmas of the same year the chapel was dedicated, and the new residence, together with St. Aloysius's school, on Congress Street, were ready for occupation before the winter's snow was gone."

The Immaculate Conception of the Blessed Virgin, Mother of God Cathedral was finished three years later, but the church suffered one more blow before the building could open for worship. "On the very night of the dedication," said Healy, "a fearful wind prostrated the lofty spire of the cathedral." High winds blew the steeple clear across the street, where it smashed into a rooftop. Luckily no one was killed. Again the bishop and his

Cumberland County Courthouse, circa 1850. *Courtesy of the Portland Public Library Special Collections and Archives.*

flock worked hard to rebuild, and according to Healy, "very soon the loftiest spire of the city crowned the finest church in the state of Maine."

Healy also talked about the current state of his church in 1886, when the Catholic population had grown to about nine thousand in Portland. Though still a minority, he subtly urged the Catholics to flex their political muscle. "Let our fellow citizens bear in mind," he said, "that in our schools we have one thousand children, whose education costs the city nothing." He also encouraged them to feel proud of their heritage. "Forget not what you represent," he exhorted them, "the Church of old, the church which made Christians of the Abenaki before Portland was founded…We are not of yesterday here or elsewhere. As Catholics we have a prior claim to be here as citizens."

Healy spoke with pride and a bit of defiance as a member of a minority religion, a Catholic in a city dominated by Protestants. But underlying that was the minority status he kept to himself and the racial inequity that had molded his life. He was still speaking for Catholics when he concluded that "we ask but our just and equal rights." But as the son of a slave, his words resonated far beyond the walls of the cathedral.

The Best Celebration

Strange to me now are the forms I meet
When I visit the dear old town;
But the native air is pure and sweet,
And the trees that o'ershadow each well-known street,
As they balance up and down,
Are singing the beautiful song,
Are sighing and whispering still:
"A boy's will is the wind's will,
And the thoughts of youth are long, long thoughts."
–Henry Wadsworth Longfellow, "My Lost Youth"

The signal guns resounded through the city streets at precisely 10:30 a.m.. The bands began to play, and the procession began its slow way down Congress Street, with nearly every cross street adding another contingent. At noon, the warships in the harbor fired a salute as the final group, the steamroller machine and its crew, added themselves to the line. Twenty-five thousand visitors crowded along sidewalks, grandstands and front steps of commercial buildings, while the younger ones perched on fences and posts. The whole town of Portland seemed to parade past, reenacting the city's history in a series of tableaux displayed in a new way: mounted on wheeled conveyances called "floats."

The natives sat before their wigwams, Cleeve and Tucker built a log house, a stagecoach delivered the mail and Mowatt sailed his sloop of war into harbor, the scenes frozen in time as the floats rolled by. Seven hundred schoolchildren

Statue of Thomas Brackett Reed. *Photograph by Kate Johnson.*

marched carrying banners from every city school. The allegorical cars were next, drawn by plumed horses and featuring the Goddess of Liberty, the Queen of Song, the Queen of Harvest and the Flower Queen. Next came the civic bodies: the Odd Fellows, Knights of Pythias, Wheel Club, Yacht Club, Bar Association, board of trade and more. The tradesmen followed—the railways, sugar refineries, shoe manufacturers, packing companies and lumber dealers—followed by the fire department and the Norway Band. Finally the Street Department brought up the rear with its powerful new steamroller.

Both visitors and townspeople agreed that it had been the most magnificent procession the city had ever seen. It was a great day for Portland, but the city's centennial festivities had just begun. Amid red, white and blue bunting, streamers and American flags decorating nearly every façade in sight, revelers continued their celebration. Inscriptions commemorated important sites. The sign on the Grand Trunk Railway yard identified it as the place where George Cleeve first built his house. The Grand Trunk Railway Station now stood where the French and Indians had massacred settlers in 1690. The Portland Company sign on Fore Street noted that it was the site of the first meetinghouse. The Casco Bank building was built where Commodore Preble had once lived and died. On Congress Street, the house where Henry Wadsworth Longfellow had grown up was still standing.

"Centennial." From *Centennial Celebration*.

In the afternoon, vendors roamed through the crowds, selling toys, ice cream and lemonade of all colors. In Lincoln Park, Professor C.H. Grimley slowly inflated his great balloon with gas. Hundreds of schoolchildren sang patriotic songs in Deering Park, and Chandler's band played marching tunes.

As the afternoon grew late, hundreds gathered to see the great balloon ascend into the heavens. But fog had been steadily drifting in from the sea, and it quickly obscured the balloon from view.

In the evening, the crowds flocked to Bramhall Hill, where fog continued to hinder the proceedings. The historical reenactment planned for the occasion was performed on schedule. It involved a lengthy portrayal

City hall, circa 1870. *Courtesy of the Portland Public Library Special Collections and Archives.*

of battles between the Indians and early settlers that had taken place in Portland's wilder past. The entire drama was performed, culminating in the massacre at Fort Loyal in which twenty-five settlers were killed by townspeople portraying Indians. The script for the reenactment called for war dancing, attacking, scalp dancing, besieging, capturing and burning by the Indians and their French allies, as well as much building and rebuilding by the hapless settlers. However, the eager spectators could see very little of this through the thickening fog. The fireworks, scheduled to follow, had to be postponed.

The hotels were bustling that night, the Preble House, the Eagle and the Falmouth all proudly offering their state-of-the-art accommodations to out-of-town guests. The festivities continued on Tuesday, with all kinds of boats races from Union Wharf to Great Eastern Wharf and back. Single scull, four oars, working boats and juniors all had their competitions, with generous cash prizes of upward to seventy-five dollars, gold watches, silver watches and opera glasses to the winners. Then crowds flocked to city hall, where Mayor Charles Chapman pronounced the "genius" of the past century to be the country's, and Portland's, "material and moral development." Local

Corner of Middle and Exchange Street. From *Portland and Vicinity.*

attorney Thomas Brackett Reed gave a long speech detailing the history of Portland, followed by an equally lengthy epic poem by Abba Goold Woolson. After so much speechifying and versifying, participants happily left city hall and proceeded to the customhouse wharf, where they boarded steamers for Long Island. In unusually warm ninety-degree weather, some two thousand people milled around the sixteen cords of burning wood, watching the clams and lobsters cook, and then seated themselves at an acre of tables to consume lobsters and nearly three hundred bushels of clams.

Returning to the mainland, it was back to city hall once again for evening exercises. Some of Portland's native sons who had distinguished themselves in the wider world entertained the audience until Reverend Hugh Carpenter ended the day with the observation that "I think you have had about enough oratory, enough poetry, enough marching and, some of you, probably even enough clams."

Many said that Portland's centennial had been the best celebration that had ever occurred in the city. Finally, on Wednesday, it was capped off with the postponed fireworks display on the Western Promenade. On the warm summer night, spectators watched gold clouds studded with sapphires, peacock plumes, flying pigeons, floral fountains and more burst into light in the sky above the bay. Portland's centennial celebration had served as a homecoming for former residents and ancestors of former residents who had returned to the city by the sea, the setting for their childhood memories or for the long-ago stories told by their parents and grandparents, stories of simpler times and stories of struggles. The finale of the fireworks display celebrated them all as the city's coat of arms illuminated the sky, a grand flight of five hundred multicolored rockets exploded at once, forming a grand aerial bouquet, and colored lights spelled out the words "Welcome Sons of Portland."

Bibliography

Albright, Raymond W. *A History of the Protestant Episcopal Church.* New York: Macmillan Company, 1964.

Ash, Deborah Lyttle. "Tinware, Painted." *Encyclopedia of American Folkart.* New York: Routledge, 2004.

Baxter, James Phinney, ed. *Documentary History of the State of Maine.* Vol. 3. Portland, ME: Maine Historical Society, 1884.

Bentley, G.E., Jr. "The Freaks of Learning." *Colby Quarterly*, June 1982.

Bowne, Eliza. *A Girl's Life Eighty Years Ago.* New York: Charles Scribner's & Sons, 1888.

Collections of the Maine Historical Society. Vol. 3, Portland, ME: Maine Historical Society, 1853.

Craft, William. *Running a Thousand Miles for Freedom.* London: William Tweedy, 1860.

Cutter, William Richard, ed. *Genealogical and Personal Memoirs.* Vol. 2. Easter, MA: Lewis Historical Publishing Company, 1908.

Eastern Argus. October 1860. John M. Adams, editor.

———. September 1807. Nathaniel Willis, editor.

Elwell, Edward Henry. *Portland and Vicinity.* Portland, ME: Loring, Short and Harmon, 1881.

Goold, William. *Portland in the Past.* Portland, ME: B. Thurston and Company, 1886.

Hubbard, William. *A Narrative of the Indian Wars in New England.* Stockbridge, MA: Heman Willard, 1677.

Hull, John T., ed. *Centennial Celebration: An Account of the Municipal Celebration of the One Hundredth Anniversary of the Incorporation of the Town of Portland.* Portland, ME: Owen, Strout & Company, 1886.

Ilsley, Charles P. "School Boys of Fifty Years Ago." *Portland Sunday Times*, August 1875.

London, Joshua E. *Victory in Tripoli.* Hoboken, NJ: John Wiley and Sons, Inc., 2005.

Martin, Gina, and Lois Tucker. "American Painted Tinware." Historical Society of Early American Decoration, Cooperstown, New York, 2007.

Mather, Cotton. "An Appendix Containing an History of Some Criminals Executed in New England for Capital Crimes." *The Ecclesiastical History of New England.* Hartford, CT: Silas Andrus and Son, 1853.

McClellan, Hugh. *History of Gorham, Maine.* Portland, ME: Smith and Sales, 1903.

McKee, Christopher. *Edward Preble: A Naval Biography.* Annapolis, MD: U.S. Naval Institute Press, 1996.

Moulton, Augustus F. *Portland by the Sea.* Augusta, ME: Katahdin Publishing Company, 1926.

Neal, John. *Portland Illustrated.* Portland, ME: W.S. Jones, 1874.

New York Times. Articles from 1861 and 1862.

Portland City Guide. Sponsored by the City of Portland. Portland, ME: Forest City Printing Company, 1940.

Portland Gazette. 1805. Isaac Adams and William Jenks, editors.

———. 1798–1805. Eleazer A. Jenks, editor.

Preble, George Henry. *Genealogical Sketch of the First Three Generations of the Prebles in America.* Boston, MA: David Clapp and Sons, 1808.

Sassicier, Agnes L. "Painted Tin or Tole." Old and Sold. oldandsold.com. http://www.oldandsold.com/articles01/article732.shtml.

Schriver, Edward O. "Go Free: The Antislavery Impulse in Maine." University of Maine Studies, 1970, Orono, Maine.

Soodalter, Ron. *Hanging Captain Gordon.* New York: Atria Books, 2006.

Sylvester, Herbert Milton. *Indian Wars of New England: The Land of the Abenake.* Boston, MA: W.B. Clarke Company, 1910.

Todd, John M. *A Sketch of the Life of John M. Todd.* Portland, ME: William W. Roberts Company, 1906.

Willis, William. *The History of Portland, From 1632 to 1864.* 2nd ed. Portland, ME: Bailey & Noyes, 1865.

Willis William, ed. *Journals of the Rev. Thomas Smith and the Rev. Samuel Deane.* Portland, ME: Joseph S. Bailey, 1849.

Winthrop, John. *The History of New England from 1630 to 1649.* Boston, MA: Phelps and Farnham, 1825.

Index

N

P

Q

R

S

T

U

W

Y

About the Author

Luann teaches writing classes at the University of Maine at Farmington. Her first book, *Remembering Franklin County*, was published by The History Press in 2009.